PATHWAYS

Reading, Writing, and Critical Thinking

3A

Mari Vargo   Laurie Blass

NATIONAL GEOGRAPHIC LEARNING | CENGAGE Learning

Australia • Brazil • Japan • Korea • Mexico • Singapore • Spain • United Kingdom • United States

Pathways Split Text 3A
Reading, Writing, and Critical Thinking
Mari Vargo and Laurie Blass

Publisher: Andrew Robinson
Executive Editor: Sean Bermingham
Senior Development Editor: Bill Preston
Assistant Editor: Vivian Chua
Contributing Writer: Meredith Pike-Baky
Contributing Editors: Sylvia Bloch,
 Zaneta Heng
Director of Global Marketing: Ian Martin
Marketing Manager: Emily Stewart
Director of Content and Media Production:
 Michael Burggren
Senior Content Project Manager: Daisy Sosa
Manufacturing Buyer: Marybeth Hennebury
Associate Manager, Operations:
 Leila Hishmeh
Cover Design: Page 2, LLC
Cover Image: Skip Brown/National Geographic
Interior Design: Page 2, LLC
Composition: Page 2, LLC

© 2014 National Geographic Learning, a part of Cengage Learning

ALL RIGHTS RESERVED. No part of this work covered by the copyright herein may be reproduced, transmitted, stored or used in any form or by any means graphic, electronic, or mechanical, including but not limited to photocopying, recording, scanning, digitizing, taping, Web distribution, information networks, or information storage and retrieval systems, except as permitted under Section 107 or 108 of the 1976 United States Copyright Act, without the prior written permission of the publisher.

For product information and technology assistance, contact us at
Cengage Learning Asia Customer Support, 65-6410-1200
For permission to use material from this text or product,
submit all requests online at **www.cengageasia.com/permissions**
Further permissions questions can be emailed to
asia.permissionrequest@cengage.com

ISBN 13: 978-1-285-45705-5
ISBN 10: 1-285-45705-6

Cengage Learning Asia Pte Ltd
151 Lorong Chuan #02-08
New Tech Park (Lobby H)
Singapore 556741

National Geographic Learning
20 Channel Center Street
Boston, MA 02210
USA

Cengage Learning is a leading provider of customized learning solutions with office locations around the globe, including Singapore, the United Kingdom, Australia, Mexico, Brazil, and Japan. Locate your local office at:
ngl.cengage.com

Cengage Learning products are represented in Canada by Nelson Education, Ltd.

Visit National Geographic Learning online at **ngl.cengage.com**
Visit our website at **www.cengageasia.com**

---

continued from p. xiv

Map and Graphs

10, 12, 32, 49, 70–71, 94–95, 102, 104, 105, 106: All National Geographic Maps

Printed in Singapore
2 3 4 5 6 17 16 15

Contents

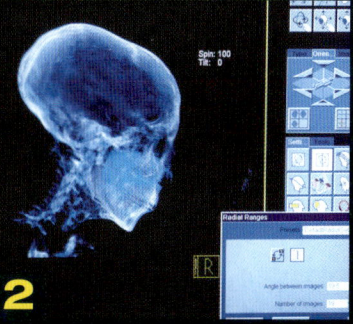

	Scope and Sequence	vi
	Explore a Unit	viii
1	Social Relationships	1
2	Science and Detection	23
3	City Solutions	47
4	Danger Zones	69
5	The Business of Tourism	93
	Video Scripts	235
	Independent Student Handbook	241
	Vocabulary and Skills Index	250

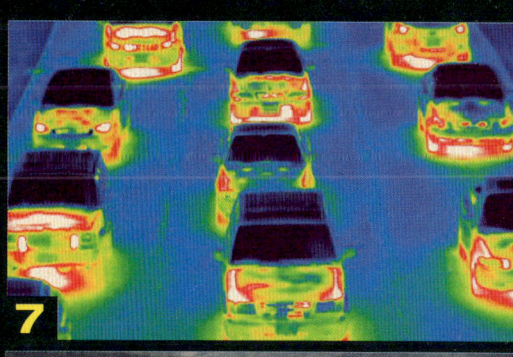
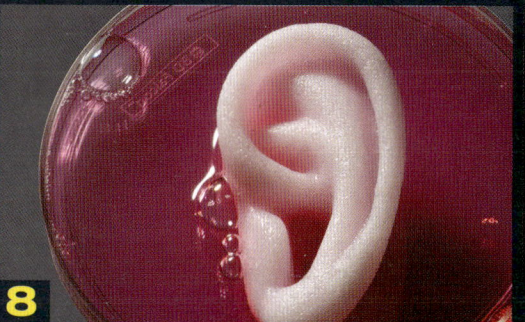

PLACES TO EXPLORE IN

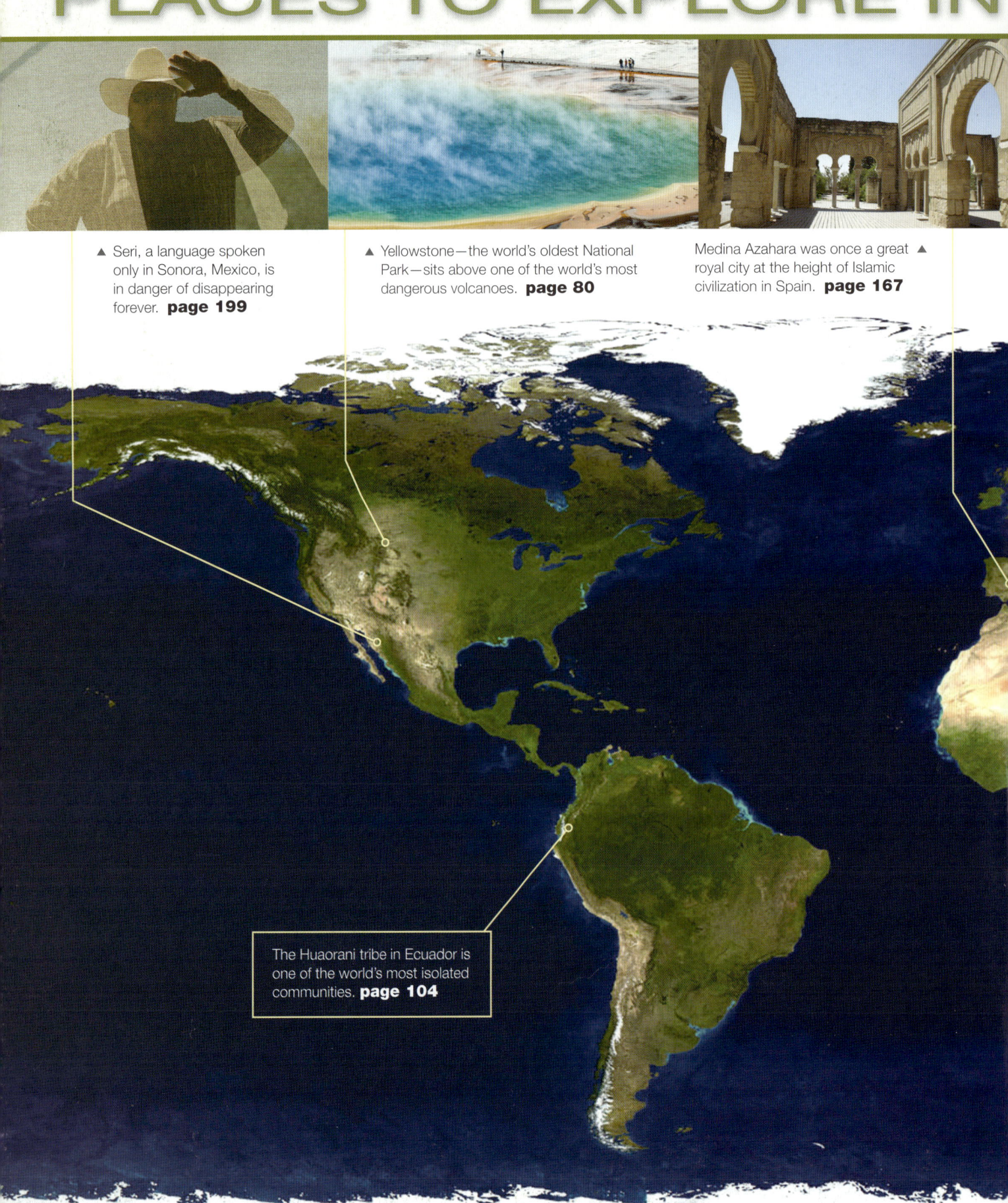

▲ Seri, a language spoken only in Sonora, Mexico, is in danger of disappearing forever. **page 199**

▲ Yellowstone—the world's oldest National Park—sits above one of the world's most dangerous volcanoes. **page 80**

Medina Azahara was once a great royal city at the height of Islamic civilization in Spain. **page 167** ▲

The Huaorani tribe in Ecuador is one of the world's most isolated communities. **page 104**

PATHWAYS

▲ In 1991, the body of the world's oldest murder victim was found in the frozen ice of the Italian Alps. **page 28**

In gelada communities, female family members have the decision-making power. **page 13** ▲

Do dense cities such as Seoul, ▲ Korea, offer the best hope for solving the world's environmental problems? **page 51**

Australia's most famous monolith, Uluru, is at the heart of a region where people have lived for over 20,000 years. **page 106**

Scope and Sequence

Unit	Academic Pathways	Vocabulary
 **1** **Social Relationships** Page 1 Academic Track: Interdisciplinary	**Lesson A:** Identifying main and supporting ideas; Evaluating supporting arguments **Lesson B:** Understanding related science news reports **Lesson C:** Reviewing paragraph writing; Writing a comparison paragraph	Understanding meaning from context; Matching words with definitions; Applying vocabulary in a personalized context; Word Partners: *cooperate*; Word Link: *pre-*
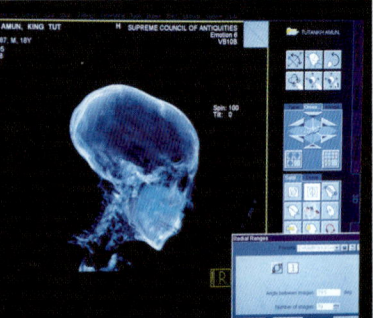 **2** **Science and Detection** Page 23 Academic Track: History/Life Science	**Lesson A:** Identifying a sequence of events; Distinguishing fact from speculation **Lesson B:** Understanding a personal narrative/opinion article **Lesson C:** Planning and writing an opinion paragraph	Understanding meaning from context; Using vocabulary to complete definitions; Applying vocabulary in a personalized context; Word Link: *extra-, com-/con-*
 **3** **City Solutions** Page 47 Academic Track: Sociology	**Lesson A:** Identifying reasons; Evaluating sources **Lesson B:** Reading an interview **Lesson C:** Writing a thesis statement; Writing descriptive paragraphs	Understanding meaning from context; Using vocabulary to complete definitions; Applying vocabulary in a personalized context; Word Partners: *income, majority*
 **4** **Danger Zones** Page 69 Academic Track: Earth Science	**Lesson A:** Organizing your notes; Analyzing and evaluating evidence **Lesson B:** Interpreting information in a multimodal text **Lesson C:** Writing an introductory paragraph; Writing opinion paragraphs	Understanding meaning from context; Matching words with definitions; Applying vocabulary in a personalized context; Word Link: *vict/vinc*; Word Partners: *tend (to)*
 **5** **The Business of Tourism** Page 93 Academic Track: Economics/Business	**Lesson A:** Analyzing causes and effects; Analyzing a writer's argument **Lesson B:** Reading related travel news reports **Lesson C:** Writing well-developed body paragraphs; Writing a short cause-effect essay	Understanding meaning from context; Matching words with definitions; Applying vocabulary in a personalized context; Word Link: *mot, dom/domin*

Reading	Writing	Viewing	Critical Thinking
Responding to text and photos Skimming to make predictions Identifying main ideas and key details Identifying supporting ideas Identifying meaning from context **Skill Focus:** Identifying main and supporting ideas	**Goal:** Writing about similarities and differences **Language:** Making comparisons **Skill:** Reviewing paragraph writing	**Video:** *Elephant Orphans* Viewing for general understanding and specific information Relating video content to a reading text	Analyzing a text to identify function Synthesizing information to identify similarities Relating ideas to personal experience **CT Focus:** Evaluating supporting arguments
Responding to text and photos Skimming to make predictions Identifying main ideas and supporting details Sequencing historical events **Skill Focus:** Identifying a sequence of events	**Goal:** Writing an opinion paragraph about research **Language:** Review of modals of obligation and possibility **Skill:** Writing an opinion paragraph	**Video:** *Columbus DNA* Viewing for general understanding and specific information Relating video content to a reading text	Interpreting evidence Inferring attitude Synthesizing information to make comparisons Analyzing a text to identify sentence types **CT Focus:** Distinguishing fact from speculation
Interpreting maps Skimming to make predictions Identifying main ideas of paragraphs Identifying supporting details and reasons Identifying meaning from context **Skill Focus:** Identifying reasons	**Goal:** Writing descriptive paragraphs about a city **Language:** Using the simple past and *used to* **Skill:** Writing a thesis statement	**Video:** *Solar Solutions* Viewing for general understanding and specific information Relating video content to a reading text	Synthesizing information and justifying an opinion Relating ideas to personal experience **CT Focus:** Evaluating sources
Interpreting map and textual information Using titles and visuals to make predictions Identifying main ideas Scanning for key details Identifying supporting ideas and reasons Understanding infographics Understanding a process **Skill Focus:** Organizing your notes	**Goal:** Writing opinion paragraphs with recommendations **Language:** Using parallel structure **Skill:** Writing an introductory paragraph	**Video:** *Hurricanes* Viewing to confirm predictions Viewing for general understanding and specific information Relating video content to reading texts	Interpreting infographics to understand a process Synthesizing information from multiple sources **CT Focus:** Analyzing and evaluating evidence
Interpreting maps and charts Predicting the content of a reading Identifying main ideas and supporting details Identifying meaning from context **Skill Focus:** Analyzing causes and effects	**Goal:** Writing a short essay about geotourism **Language:** Using If . . . (then) . . . **Skill:** Writing well-developed body paragraphs	**Video:** *Galápagos Tourism* Viewing to confirm predictions Viewing for general understanding and specific information Relating video content to reading texts	Making inferences Synthesizing information from multiple sources Relating ideas to personal experience **CT Focus:** Analyzing a writer's argument

EXPLORE A UNIT

Each unit has three lessons.
Lessons A and B develop academic reading skills and vocabulary by focusing on two aspects of the unit theme. A video section acts as a content bridge between Lessons A and B. The language and content in these sections provide the stimulus for a final writing task (Lesson C).

The **unit theme** focuses on an academic content area relevant to students' lives, such as Health Science, Business and Technology, and Environmental Science.

Academic Pathways highlight the main academic skills of each lesson.

Exploring the Theme provides a visual introduction to the unit. Learners are encouraged to think critically and share ideas about the unit topic.

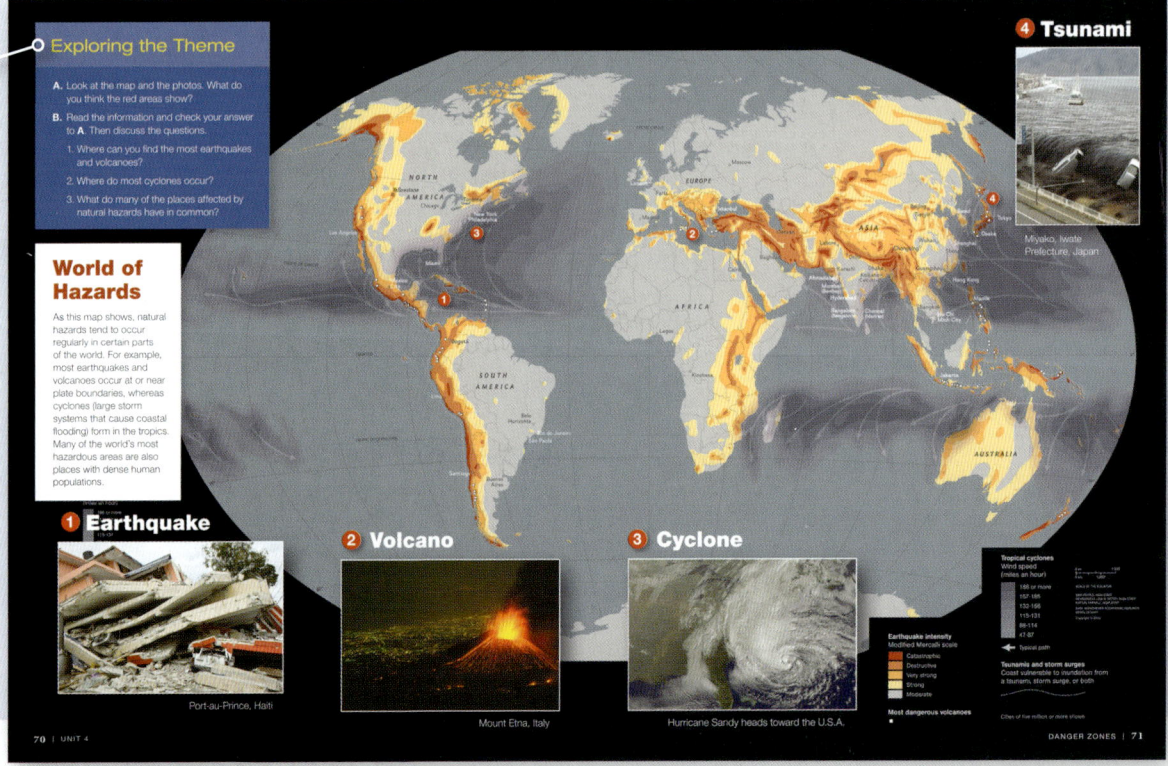

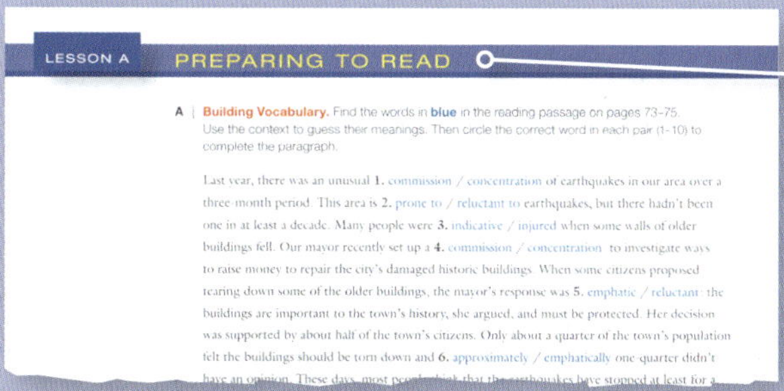

LESSON A

In **Preparing to Read**, learners are introduced to key vocabulary items from the reading passage. Lessons A and B each present and practice 10 target vocabulary items.

Reading A is a single, linear text related to the unit theme. Each reading passage is recorded on the audio program.

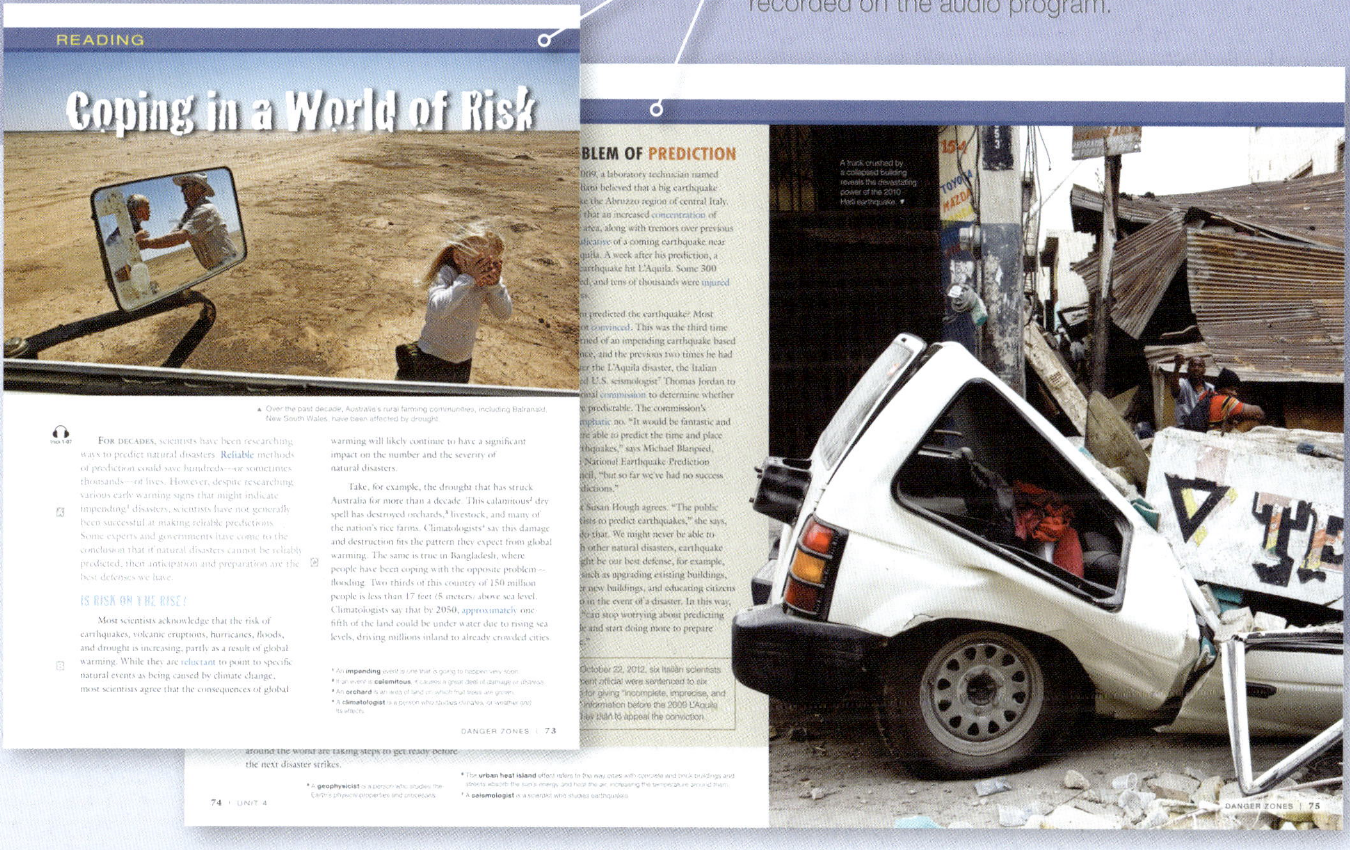

Guided comprehension tasks and reading strategy instruction enable learners to improve their academic literacy and critical thinking skills.

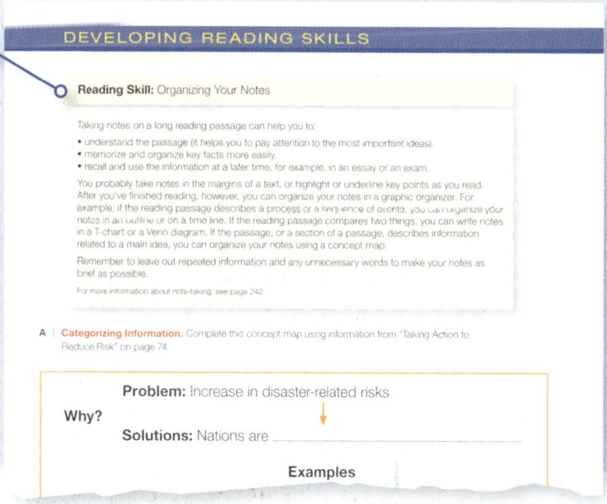

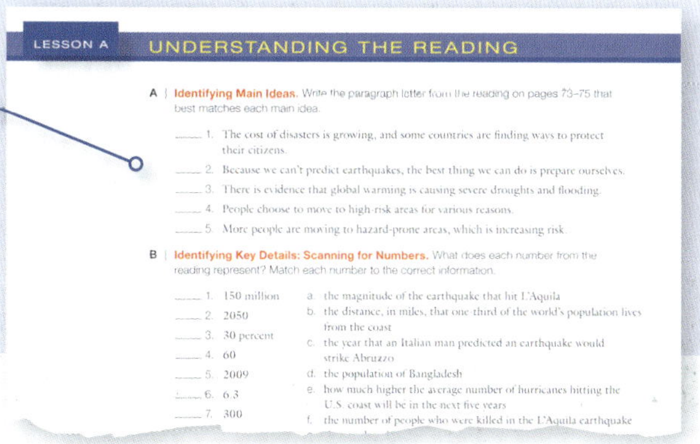

EXPLORE A UNIT | ix

EXPLORE A UNIT

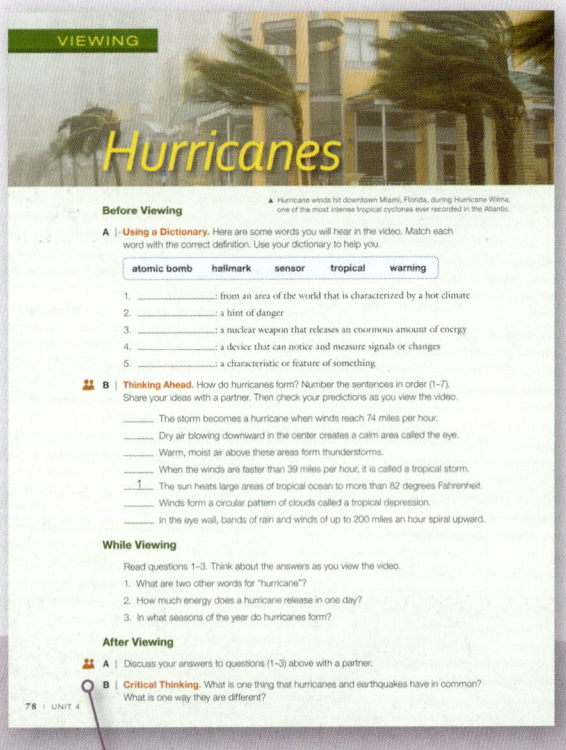

Viewing tasks related to an authentic National Geographic video serve as a content bridge between Lessons A and B. (Video scripts are on pages 233–238.)

Learners need to use their **critical thinking skills** to relate video content to information in the previous reading.

Word Link and **Word Partners** boxes develop learners' awareness of word structure, collocations, and usage.

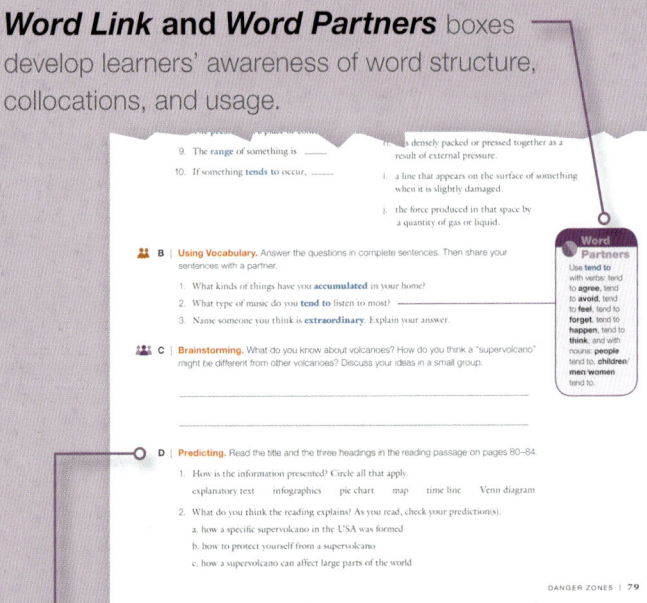

Guided pre-reading tasks and strategy tips encourage learners to think critically about what they are going to read.

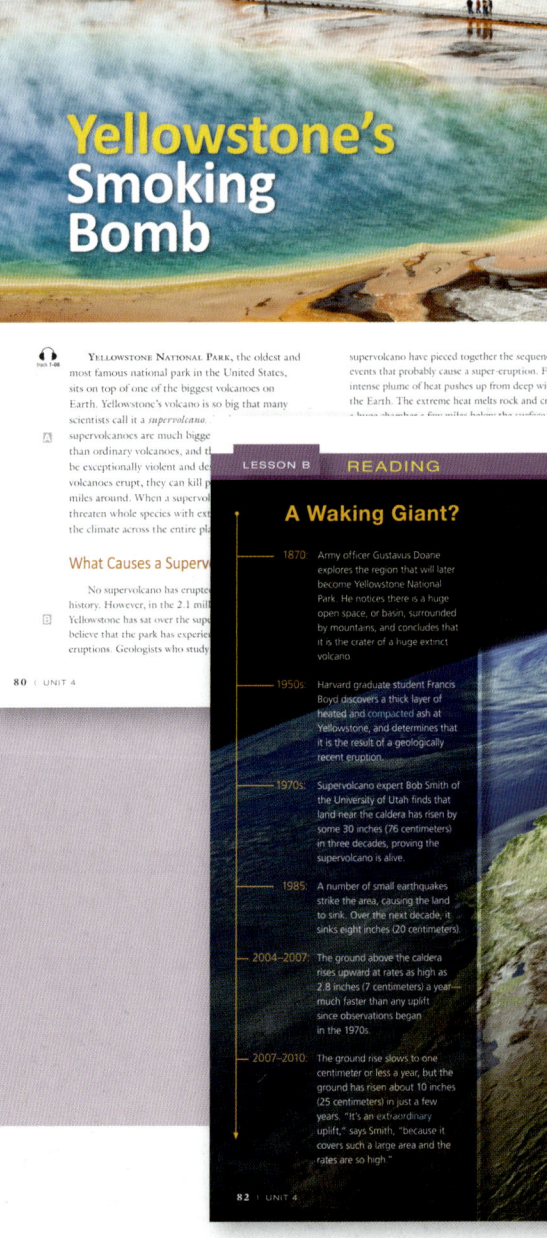

LESSON B

Lesson B's reading passage presents a further aspect of the unit theme, using a variety of text types and graphic formats.

Critical thinking tasks require learners to analyze, synthesize, and critically evaluate ideas and information in each reading.

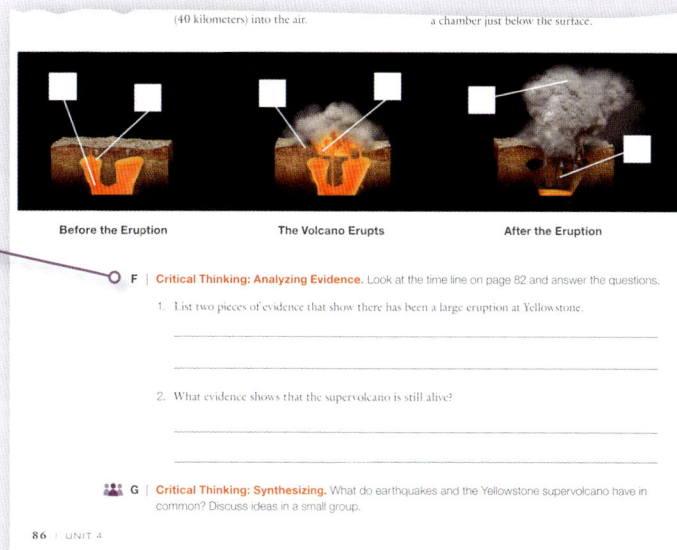

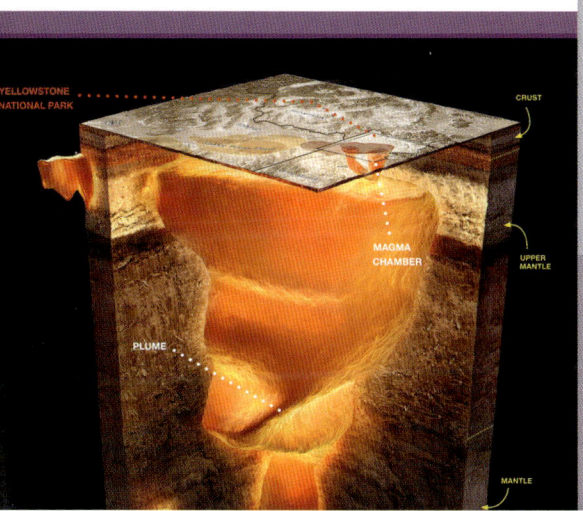

Authentic charts, maps and graphics from National Geographic support the main text, helping learners comprehend key ideas and develop visual literacy.

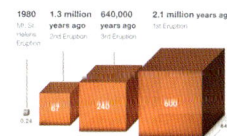

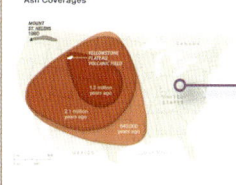

EXPLORE A UNIT

The **Goal of Lesson C** is for learners to relate their own views and experience to the theme of the unit by completing a guided writing assignment.

Integrated **grammar practice and writing skill development** provides scaffolding for the writing assignment.

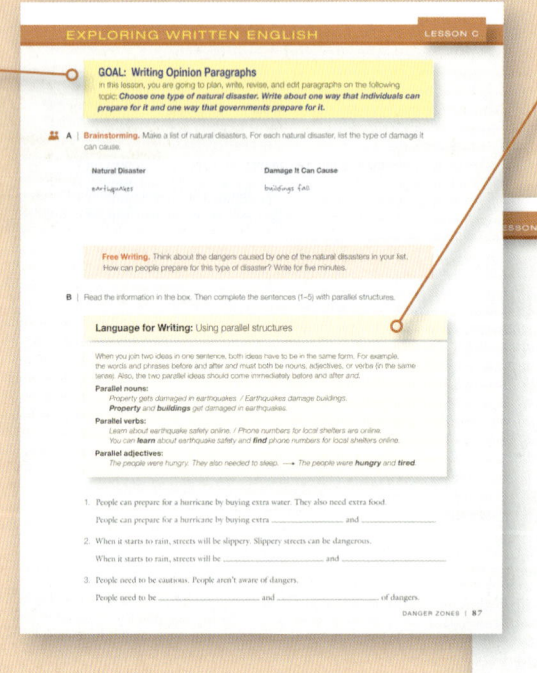
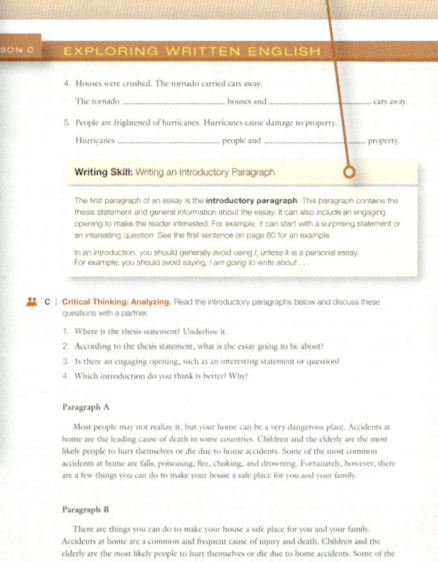

The **Independent Student Handbook** provides further language support and self-study strategies for independent learning.
▶ see pages 241–247.

Resources for *Pathways* Level 3

Teacher's Guide including teacher's notes, expansion activities, rubrics for evaluating written assignments, and answer keys for activities in the Student Book.

Video DVD with authentic National Geographic clips relating to each of the ten units.

Audio CDs with audio recordings of the Student Book reading passages.

LESSON C

A **guided process approach** develops learners' confidence in planning, drafting, revising, and editing their written work.

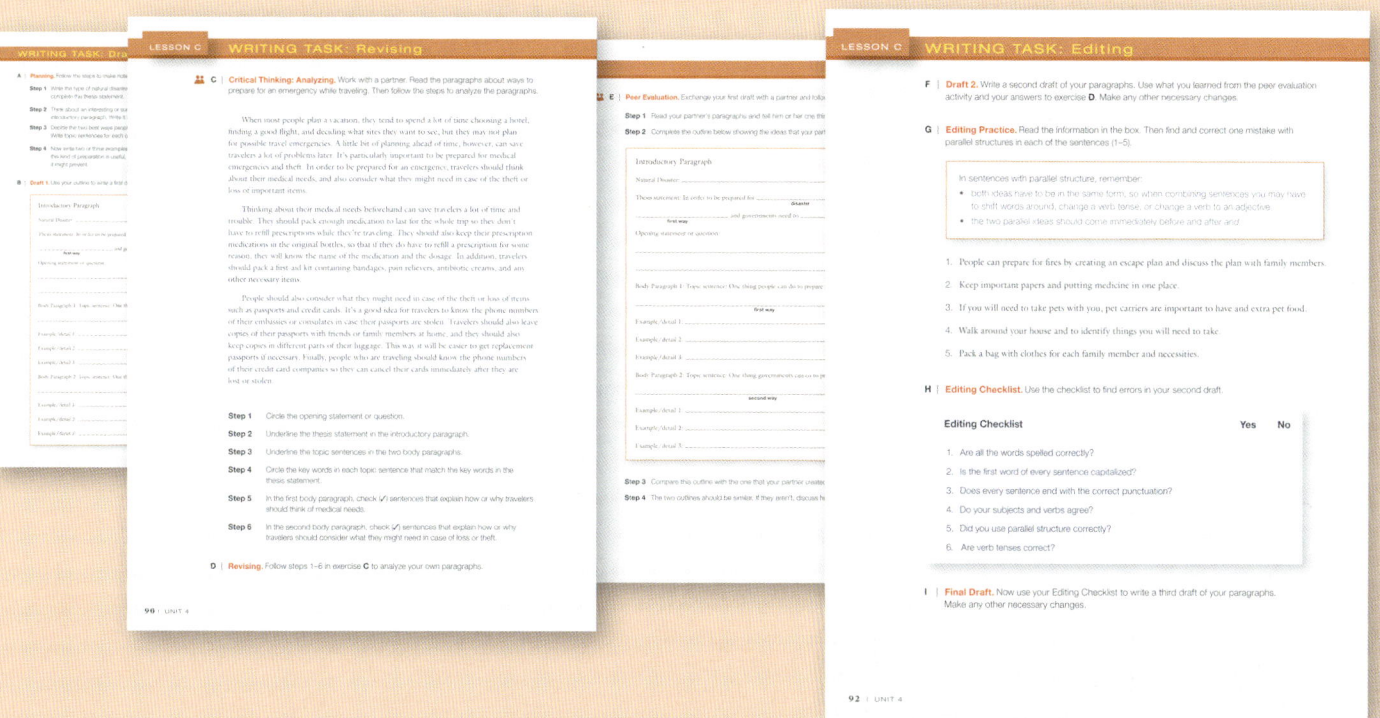

Assessment CD-ROM with ExamView® containing a bank of ready-made questions for quick and effective assessment.

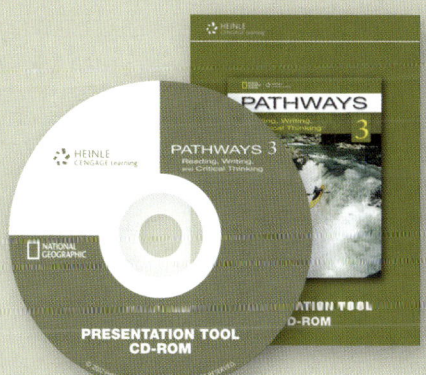

Classroom Presentation Tool CD-ROM featuring audio and video clips, and interactive activities from the Student Book. These can be used with an interactive whiteboard or computer projector.

Online Workbook, powered by MyELT, with both teacher-led and self-study options. This contains the 10 National Geographic video clips, supported by interactive, automatically graded activities that practice the skills learned in the Student Books.

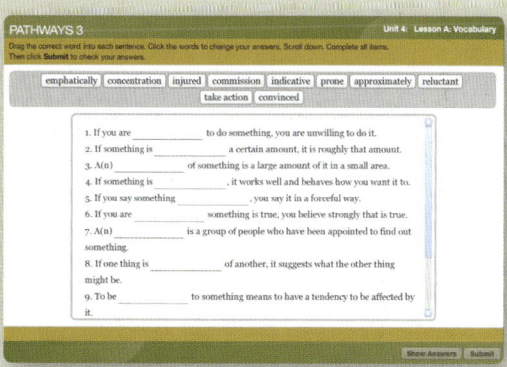

EXPLORE A UNIT | xiii

Credits

Text

5-7: Adapted from "Office Jungle Mirrors Primate Behavior," by Brian Handwerk: http://news.nationalgeographic.com/news/2005/09/0923_050923_ape_office.html, **12-14**: Adapted from "Male Bonding": http://blogs.ngm.com/blog_central/2010/06/male-bonding.html, "Kings of the Hill?" by Virginia Morrell: NGM November 2002, and "Chimp "Girls" Play With "Dolls" Too—First Wild Evidence," by Brain Handwerk: http://news.nationalgeographic.com/news/2010/09/101220-chimpanzees-play-nature-nurture-science-animals-evolution/, **27-29:** Adapted from "Crime-Fighting Leech Fingers Perp": http://news.nationalgeographic.com/news/2009/10/091020-leech-robber-dna-video-ap.html, "Animal DNA Becoming Crucial CSI Clue": http://news.nationalgeographic.com/news/2006/12/061212-animals-CSI_2.html, and "Iceman Autopsy," by Stephen S. Hall: NGM November 201, **34-38:** Adapted from "King Tut's Family Secrets," by Zahi Hawass: NGM September 2010, **51-53:** Adapted from "City Solutions," by Robert Kunzig: NGM December 2011, **59-61** Adapted from "Urban Visionary: One on One," by Keith Bellows: http://travel.nationalgeographic.com/travel/traveler-magazine/one-on-one/urban-visionary/, **73-75:** Adapted from "Coping in a World of Risk," by Peter Miller: NGM Special Issue: Nature's Fury 2010, **80-84:** Adapted from "When Yellowstone Explodes," by Joel Achenbach: NGM August 2009, **97-99:** Adapted from "One on One: Jonathan Tourtellot," by Keith Bellows: National Geographic Traveler November 2006, **104-106:** Adapted from "Moi Enomenga": http://www.nationalgeographic.com/explorers/bios/moi-enomenga/, "3 Sisters Adventure Trekking": http://www.3sistersadventure.com/, and "Australia Through Aboriginal Eyes," by Francis Wilkins: http://news.nationalgeographic.com/news/2004/12/1210_041210_travel_australia.html

NGM = National Geographic Magazine

Photo and Illustration

Cover: Skip Brown/National Geographic, **IFC:** Alison Wright/National Geographic, **IFC:** Courtesy of Empowering Women of Nepal, **IFC:** Courtesy of Max Salomon, **IFC:** Mark Theissen/National Geographic Stock, **IFC:** Courtesy of K. David Harrison, **IFC:** Courtesy of Danny Saltzman, **IFC:** Michael Nichols/National Geographic, **IFC:** Courtesy of Susan Hough, **IFC:** Mark Theissen/National Geographic Stock, **IFC:** Kenneth Garrett/National Geographic, **i:** Randy Olson/National Geographic, **iii:** Michael Nichols/National Geographic, **iii:** Kenneth Garrett/ National Geographic, **iii:** Jodi Cobb/National Geographic, **iii:** Sarah Leen/National Geographic Image Collection, **iii:** Ralph Lee Hopkins/National Geographic, **iii:** Medford Taylor/National Geographic, **iii:** Tyrone Turner/National Geographic, **iii:** Rebecca Hale/National Geographic, **iii:** Lynn Johnson/National Geographic, **iii:** Robert Madden/National Geographic, **iv:** Lynn Johnson/National Geographic, **iv:** Rich Reid/National Geographic, **iv:** rosesmith/Shutterstock.com, **iv-v:** NASA Goddard Space Flight Center Image by Reto Stöckli (land surface, shallow water, clouds), **v:** Kenneth Garrett/National Geographic, **v:** Michael Nichols/National Geographic, **v:** Sungjin Kim/National Geographic, **v:** Nicole Duplaix/National Geographic, **vi:** Michael Fay/National Geographic, **vi:** Kenneth Garrett/National Geographic, **vi:** Randy Olson/National Geographic, **vi:** Alison Wright/National Geographic, **vi:** Catherine Karnow/National Geographic, **1:** Paul Sutherland/National Geographic, **2-3:** Tim Laman/National Geographic, **2 (bottom):** Robert E. Hynes/National Geographic, **5:** Michael Nichols/National Geographic, **6:** Dmitriy Shironosov/ Shutterstock.com, **7:** Michael Nichols/National Geographic, **10:** NG Photographer/National Geographic Stock, **11:** Michael Nichols/National Geographic, **12:** Michael Fay/National Geographic, **13:** Michael Nichols/National Geographic, **14:** Michael Poliza/National Geographic, **23:** Kenneth Garrett/National Geographic, **24-25:** Kenneth Garrett/National Geographic, **25:** NGM Art/National Geographic, **25:** Nina Berman/National Geographic Image Collection, **25:** Sean Gallagher/National Geographic, **27:** Kenneth Garrett/National Geographic, **27:** Jason Edwards/National Geographic, **28:** Walter A. Weber/National Geographic, **29:** Kazuhiko Sano/National Geographic, **32:** Michael Hanson/National Geographic Image Collection, **32:** Tony Woodland/National Geographic My Shot/National Geographic, **34:** Kenneth Garrett/National Geographic, **35:** Kenneth Garrett/National Geographic, **36 (all):** Kenneth Garrett/National Geographic, **37:** Kenneth Garrett/National Geographic, **38:** Kenneth Garrett/National Geographic, **38:** Kenneth Garrett/National Geographic, **47:** Mark Leong/National Geographic, **48-49:** Randy Olson/National Geographic, **51:** Jodi Cobb/National Geographic, **52:** Justin Guariglia/National Geographic, **52:** John Tomanio/National Geographic, **53:** Sungjin Kim/National Geographic, **57:** Michael Poliza/National Geographic, **59:** Courtesy of Danny Saltzman, **60:** Lynn Johnson/National Geographic, **61:** Mihai-Bogdan Lazar/Shutterstock.com, **61:** Jodi Cobb/National Geographic, **69:** Sarah Leen/National Geographic Image Collection, **70:** Alison Wright/National Geographic, **70:** Carsten Peter/National Geographic Image Collection, **71:** NASA Images, **71:** © 2012 Getty Images Inc/National Geographic Image Collection, **73:** ©2009/Amy Toensing/National Geographic Image Collection, **75:** Alison Wright/National Geographic, **78:** Mike Theiss/National Geographic Stock, **80:** Rich Reid/National Geographic, **81:** Hernan Canellas/National Geographic Image Collection, **82-83:** Hernan Canellas/National Geographic, **84:** Alejandro Tumas/National Geographic, **86:** Hernan Canellas/National Geographic Image Collection, **93:** Kent Kobersteen/National Geographic, **95:** Catherine Karnow/National Geographic, **97:** Ralph Lee Hopkins/National Geographic, **98:** Mark Theissen/National Geographic Stock, **98-99:** Richard Nowitz/National Geograph, **102:** Ralph Lee Hopkins/National Geographic Stock, **104:** Mark Theissen/National Geographic Stock, **105:** Photo courtesy of Lisa Clark, **106:** Richard Nowitz/National Geographic, **241:** Elizabeth Stevens/National Geographic, **254:** Ralph Lee Hopkins/National Geographic Stock

Social Relationships

UNIT 1

ACADEMIC PATHWAYS

Lesson A: Identifying main and supporting ideas
Evaluating supporting arguments
Lesson B: Understanding related science news reports
Lesson C: Reviewing paragraph writing
Writing a comparison paragraph

Think and Discuss

1. What roles do males and females play in human society?
2. Are there similarities between the roles humans play and the roles some male and female animals play?

▲ A baby western lowland gorilla shares a grass meal with its half brother at the National Zoological Park, Washington, D.C.

Tourists watch a group of snow monkeys relaxing in a hot spring in Nagano Prefecture, Japan.

A **primate** is a member of the group of mammals that includes humans, monkeys, and apes. The largest **apes**—known as "great apes"— include gorillas, bonobos, orangutans, and chimpanzees.

Exploring the Theme

Read the information on these pages and discuss the questions.

1. What are some examples of nonhuman primates?
2. What similarities have researchers discovered between humans and other primates?
3. What are some other possible similarities between humans and other primates?

Social Animals

Researchers have discovered that humans share some behavioral characteristics with other primates. For example, primatologists—scientists who study primates—have found that some apes are capable of basic communication using human sign language. Primatologists have also observed apes inventing and using tools to get food and complete other tasks.

In addition, because both humans and primates tend to live in social groups, they may share some characteristics in terms of their social behavior. Researchers today are looking at the similarities and differences in how humans and animals interact within their own social groups, for example, the roles that each member plays within a family.

LESSON A | PREPARING TO READ

A | Building Vocabulary. Find the words in **blue** in the reading passage on pages 5–7. Use the context (the words around them) to guess their meanings. Then write the correct word from the box to complete each sentence (1–10).

> 7 conflict   4 cooperate   10 distribution   3 dynamics   1 function
> 2 hierarchy   6 perception   8 reveal   5 role   9 status

1. If people _____ as a group, they work together for a specific purpose.
2. A _____ is a way or system of organizing people into different levels of importance.
3. The _____ of a situation are forces in the situation that cause it to change.
4. If you _____ with someone, you work with or help them.
5. The _____ of someone or something is the part the person or thing plays in a particular situation.
6. Your _____ of something is the way you think about it or the impression you have of it.
7. A _____ is a serious disagreement or fight.
8. To _____ something is to make people aware of it.
9. An individual's _____ is the importance that other individuals give him or her.
10. The _____ of something is the way that is shared among a group, or spread over an area.

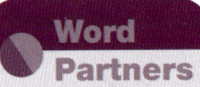

Word Partners
Use **cooperate** with: *(v.)* **agree to** cooperate, **continue to** cooperate, **fail to** cooperate, **refuse to** cooperate; *(adv.)* cooperate **fully**; *(n.)* **willingness to** cooperate.

B | Using Vocabulary. Answer the questions. Share your ideas with a partner.

1. Who do you usually **cooperate** with in your daily life? In what ways do you cooperate?
2. How can people avoid **conflict**? Give an example.
3. How has the Internet changed the **distribution** of information?

C | Brainstorming. Discuss your answers to these questions in small groups.
What are the benefits of cooperation in the workplace? How does cooperating with others help office workers? Do any animals that you are familiar with cooperate with each other? Which ones?

D | Predicting. Quickly skim the reading passage on pages 5–7 and answer these questions. Then, as you read the passage, check your predictions.

1. What two groups does the passage focus on? _____
2. What is the reading passage mainly about? _____

4 | UNIT 1

READING

THE APE IN THE OFFICE

A **DOES THE "OFFICE JUNGLE"** mirror behavior in the real jungle? New research suggests business leaders and corporate employees may use conflict and cooperation in ways similar to their primate relatives.

B In his book *The Ape in the Corner Office: Understanding the Workplace Beast in All of Us*, science writer Richard Conniff examines corporate behavior through the eyes of a primatologist.[1] Conniff, a specialist in animal behavior, suggests that the ways in which humans manage conflict and cooperation are key to their successes or failures—just like primates. He sees similarities in the ways humans and primates use social networks and hierarchies to assert and gain status in their respective groups. He also points out that while conflict can be effective at times, both humans and apes generally prefer to cooperate with each other.

COOPERATION VS. CONFLICT

C People often have the perception that the animal world is full of conflict. However, while conflict and aggression are normal primate behaviors, they actually play a more limited social role in the wild than cooperation. In fact, according to Conniff, both primates and humans are essentially social creatures. They thrive in groups and are normally cooperative and helpful. Within their own group, people generally live in harmony[2] and offer each other support. Similarly, chimpanzees live cooperatively and normally try to avoid conflict. They typically spend their days caring for their young, and traveling together in small groups. Conniff points out that chimps, despite having a reputation for being aggressive, only spend about five percent of the day displaying antagonistic[3] behaviors. In contrast, they spend much more time—15 to 20 percent of the day—grooming each other. For humans and primates, conflict is infrequent and does not last long. For both species, cooperation is a more effective way to succeed and survive.

[1] A **primatologist** is a scientist who studies primates, the group of mammals that includes humans, monkeys, and apes.
[2] If you **live in harmony** with others, you live peacefully with them rather than fighting or arguing with them.
[3] If your behavior is **antagonistic**, you act in an angry, aggressive, or unfriendly way.

SOCIAL RELATIONSHIPS | 5

▲ Aggressive behavior in the office may bring results, but it also leads to isolation for the aggressor.

THE VALUE OF NETWORKING

Research by primatologists also reveals that people and primates use similar social networking strategies to get ahead in life. They create tight social bonds by sharing resources, doing each other favors, building teams, and making friends. Employees with ambitious career goals, for example, often rely on powerful and influential people in their office to help them get better jobs. In a similar way, chimps work to strengthen relationships with other chimps. Frans de Waal, a primatologist at Emory University's Yerkes National Primate Research Center in Atlanta, Georgia, claims that if you're a chimp, "you can never reach a high position in their world if you don't have friends who help you." In fact, research shows that chimps often scheme to create bonds to strengthen their status, or importance, in the community. They do favors for one another, share resources, and sometimes use their cunning.[4] "In chimps a common strategy is to break up alliances that can be used against them," de Waal explains. "They see a main rival sitting with someone else and they try to break up [that meeting]. They use strategies that I'm sure most people perform without knowing that they are doing them."

THE IMPORTANCE OF HIERARCHIES

Groups in an office environment have similar social dynamics to groups in primate communities. In both cases, the groups organize themselves into natural and effective hierarchies in which individual members know their roles. For both humans and apes, individuals have a relative order of importance, or status, in a group. Their rank, or position in relation to other group members, largely determines their behavior. For example, young people may bow to elders, and speak softly as they look away when addressing people with higher status. People with lower status generally smile more, as they worry about pleasing people with higher status. Similarly, Conniff explains that when chimpanzees approach a powerful or senior member, they appear to reduce their body size and make themselves look as small as they can. In most primate societies, de Waal notes, social hierarchies determine the distribution

[4] **Cunning** is the ability to achieve things in a clever way, often by deceiving other people.

▲ Chest-pounding is a sign of aggression among gorillas, such as these adults in the Republic of the Congo.

of resources such as food. Young chimps defer to more powerful members when food is scarce. While the resources may be different in an office, Conniff suggests that the same dynamics are at work. "Baboons are obsessed with who gets the best spot on the jackalberry tree.[5] We're obsessed with who's got the best BlackBerry[6] or the best office."

THE LIMITS OF AGGRESSION

Although cooperation and harmony are more common in groups, both humans and primates have strong power drives, and they sometimes introduce conflict in order to assert themselves or gain status. People sometimes shout or intimidate[7] others to make a point or win an argument. Apes show aggression by pounding their chests, screeching, or banging trees. Conflict and aggression get attention, and these behaviors show an individual's power or superiority in the group. However, Conniff notes that conflict and aggressive behavior do not gain long-term success for either species. He points out that when bosses or managers become bullies[8]—for example, by criticizing their employees, treating them unfairly, and making their working lives difficult—employees become stressed, lose motivation, and quit their jobs. For apes, aggressive behavior results in chasing other apes away. In both cases, socially aggressive behavior can result in isolation for the aggressor, and neither humans nor apes seek to be alone.

In *The Ape in the Corner Office*, Conniff makes the case that kindness and polite interaction are the more common and beneficial social behaviors for humans and primates. "The truth is we are completely dependent on other people emotionally as well as for our physical needs," Conniff concludes. "We function as part of a group rather than as individuals." Employees who cooperate in the office and primates who interact collaboratively in the wild find themselves happier, more effective, and more likely to survive.

[5] A **jackalberry tree** is a tree that grows mostly in Africa. It has purple fruit that many wild animals eat.
[6] **BlackBerry** is a brand name for a type of mobile phone.
[7] If you **intimidate** people, you deliberately make them frightened enough to do what you want them to do.
[8] **Bullies** are people who use their strength or power to hurt or frighten other people.

LESSON A — UNDERSTANDING THE READING

A | Identifying Main Ideas. Look at the first column in the chart below. Use words and phrases from the reading to complete the points of comparison (1–4) between primates and humans.

B | Identifying Key Details. Look at columns two and three in the chart. Add examples that illustrate the points of comparison (a-m) in the correct places. Some examples go in both columns.

> a. bow to elders, speak softly, and look away b. share resources c. do favors d. build teams
> e. make friends f. groom one another g. care for the young h. travel together in groups
> i. rely on powerful people to get better jobs j. shout k. pound chests, screech, or bang trees
> l. thrive in groups m. reduce body size to look smaller

Points of Comparison: Both humans in offices and primates in the wild...	Human Examples	Primate Examples
1. tend to _cooperate_ with each other and avoid _conflict_.	thrive in groups, g, h	g, h groom one another, thrive in groups,
2. use _similar social networking strategies_ to get ahead.	rely on powerful people to get better jobs, c	b, d, e, m
3. organize themselves into _natural_ and behave according to rank.	a,	m
4. sometimes use _aggressive_ behavior to assert themselves.	j	k

CT Focus

Evaluating supporting arguments

Once you identify the main points in a reading passage, ask yourself: What evidence does the writer give to support his or her main points? Is there enough supporting information? Are the writer's supporting arguments convincing?

C | Identifying Supporting Ideas. Find information in the reading passage to answer these questions. Note the letter of the paragraph where you find the answer. Discuss your answers with a partner.

1. What percentage of their day do chimps behave antagonistically?
   _5%_ Paragraph: _C_

2. What is one situation in which young chimps defer to powerful group members?
   when food is scarce Paragraph: _E_

3. Why doesn't aggression always work for either humans or primates?
   It leads to isolation Paragraph: _E_

D | Critical Thinking: Evaluating Supporting Arguments. Discuss answers to the following questions with a partner.

1. Does the article provide an equal amount of description of human and ape behavior?
2. Do you agree with the main points of "The Ape in the Office"? Why, or why not?

E | Personalizing. Can you think of examples from your own experience that either support or contradict the ideas expressed in the reading? Share yoru ideas with a partner.

DEVELOPING READING SKILLS

Reading Skill: Identifying Main and Supporting Ideas

The main idea of a paragraph is the most important idea, or the idea that the paragraph is about. Paragraphs also have supporting ideas--information that helps to explain the main idea. As you read, it is often important to identify the main ideas of paragraphs (or sections) in a passage, and to distinguish them from supporting ideas.

For example, which of these sentences best expresses the main idea in Paragraph C of "The Ape in the Office"?

a. Both primates and humans tend to spend more time being cooperative than they do fighting with each other.

b. Chimpanzees typically spend their days traveling together and taking care of each other.

Sentence **a** expresses the main idea of the paragraph. Sentence **b** expresses a supporting idea; it helps to explain the main idea by providing an example.

A | Identifying Main Ideas. Circle the letter of the sentences that express main ideas in "The Ape in the Office." Then explain your choices with a partner.

1. Paragraph D
   a. People and primates both use social connections to improve their situations.
   b. Employees often rely on powerful people in the office to help them get better jobs.

2. Paragraph E
   a. When young chimpanzees approach a senior member of the group, they often make themselves smaller.
   b. Both humans and primates organize themselves into hierarchies.

3. Paragraph F
   a. Neither humans nor primates like to be alone.
   b. Both primates and humans sometimes use aggression to show that they have power.

B | Applying. Read the following paragraph about gorilla behavior. Then read the sentences that follow. Write **M** if the sentence expresses the main idea. Write **S** if the sentence expresses a supporting idea.

   Scientists have found that male gorillas in the forests of northern Congo splash water to intimidate other males who are competing with them to find a mate. Richard Parnell, a primate researcher at the University of Stirling, studied the behavior of western lowland gorillas in swamps[1] where gorilla families come to eat. He observed that the swamp was a meeting place for males searching for females. He noted that males intimidate other males and try to get the attention of females by energetically splashing water with their hands. In one type of splashing behavior, for example, male gorillas raise one or both arms and hit the surface of the water with their palms open. Using water to intimidate other males and get the attention of females shows that gorillas are "adaptable, innovative, and intelligent creatures," Parnell concluded.

_____ Male gorillas hit the water with their palms open.

_____ Male gorillas splash water to get the attention of females and to intimidate other males.

_____ Lowland gorillas go to swamps to eat and to meet other gorillas.

[1] **Swamps** are areas of very wet land with wild plants growing in them.

VIEWING

Elephant Orphans

▲ Orphan elephants are fed with baby bottles at the David Sheldrick Wildlife Trust.

Before Viewing

A | **Using a Dictionary.** The words in **bold** are used in the video. Match each word with the correct definition. Use your dictionary to help you.

The David Sheldrick Wildlife Trust in Nairobi, Kenya, takes care of **orphan** elephants. Many of these elephants are orphans because poachers **slaughtered** their mothers. **Caretakers** at the Sheldrick Wildlife Trust stay with the orphans 24 hours a day, in order to provide them with plenty of **maternal interaction**. The goal of the Trust is the **reintroduction** of the elephants back into the wild.

1. _reintroduction_ (noun) putting something back into an environment where it once was
2. _Caretaker_ (noun) people who are responsible for taking care of animals or other people
3. _Slaughtered_ (verb) killed in a way that was cruel or unnecessary
4. _maternal_ (adjective) like a mother
5. _interaction_ (noun) communication with others
6. _Orphan_ (noun) a child whose parents are dead

B | **Thinking Ahead.** If humans take care of a baby orphaned elephant, what kind of care might it need to survive? Discuss with a partner.

While Viewing

Read questions 1–4. Think about the answers as you view the video.

1. What percentage of orphaned elephants saved by the Sheldrick Wildlife Trust survive?
2. What do baby elephants need besides food to survive?
3. What are some examples of how the caretakers try to mimic an elephant's relationship with its mother?
4. What examples does the video give of the similarities between human children and elephant children? Both human and elephant children/babies _____.

After Viewing

A | Discuss your answers to questions 1–4 above with a partner.

B | **Critical Thinking: Synthesizing.** How are primates and elephants similar?

PREPARING TO READ

LESSON B

A | **Building Vocabulary.** Find the words in **blue** in the reading passage on pages 12–14. Use the context to guess their meanings. Then match the sentence parts below to make definitions.

1. ____ If something is **intense**, e
2. ____ A **psychologist** c
3. ____ **Authority** is h
4. ____ If something is **rigid**, —strict f
5. ____ A **period** is i
6. ____ If you **establish** something, j
7. ____ "**Gender**" refers to b
8. ____ To **generate** something means —toora = produce d
9. ____ "**Previously**" means g
10. ____ If you **demonstrate** a —show a particular skill,

a. you show by your behavior that you have it.
b. the characteristics of being male or female.
c. studies the mind and the reasons for people's behavior.
d. to cause it to begin or develop.
e. it is very great or extreme in strength or degree.
f. it cannot be changed or varied.
g. before the period that you are talking about.
h. the right or power to command and control others.
i. a length of time.
j. you create it.

B | **Using Vocabulary.** Discuss these questions with a partner.

1. What **period** in your life has been the happiest so far?
2. What are some ways to **generate** ideas for a writing assignment?
3. In your opinion, are any of the rules at your school too **rigid**? Which ones?
4. What people that you know have **authority**? How do they express their authority?

Word Link
The prefix **pre-** means *before*, e.g., **pre**viously, **pre**dict, **pre**cede, **pre**fix.

C | **Predicting.** Read the title and the three headings in the reading passage on pages 12–14 and answer the question.

What links the three stories together? Circle one or more answers. As you read, check your predictions.

a. They're all about male and female roles in animal societies.
b. They're all based on scientific research of primates in Africa.
c. They're all about animal societies in which females have power.

SOCIAL RELATIONSHIPS | 11

LESSON B — READING

Gender in the Wild:
Three Studies Reveal New Findings

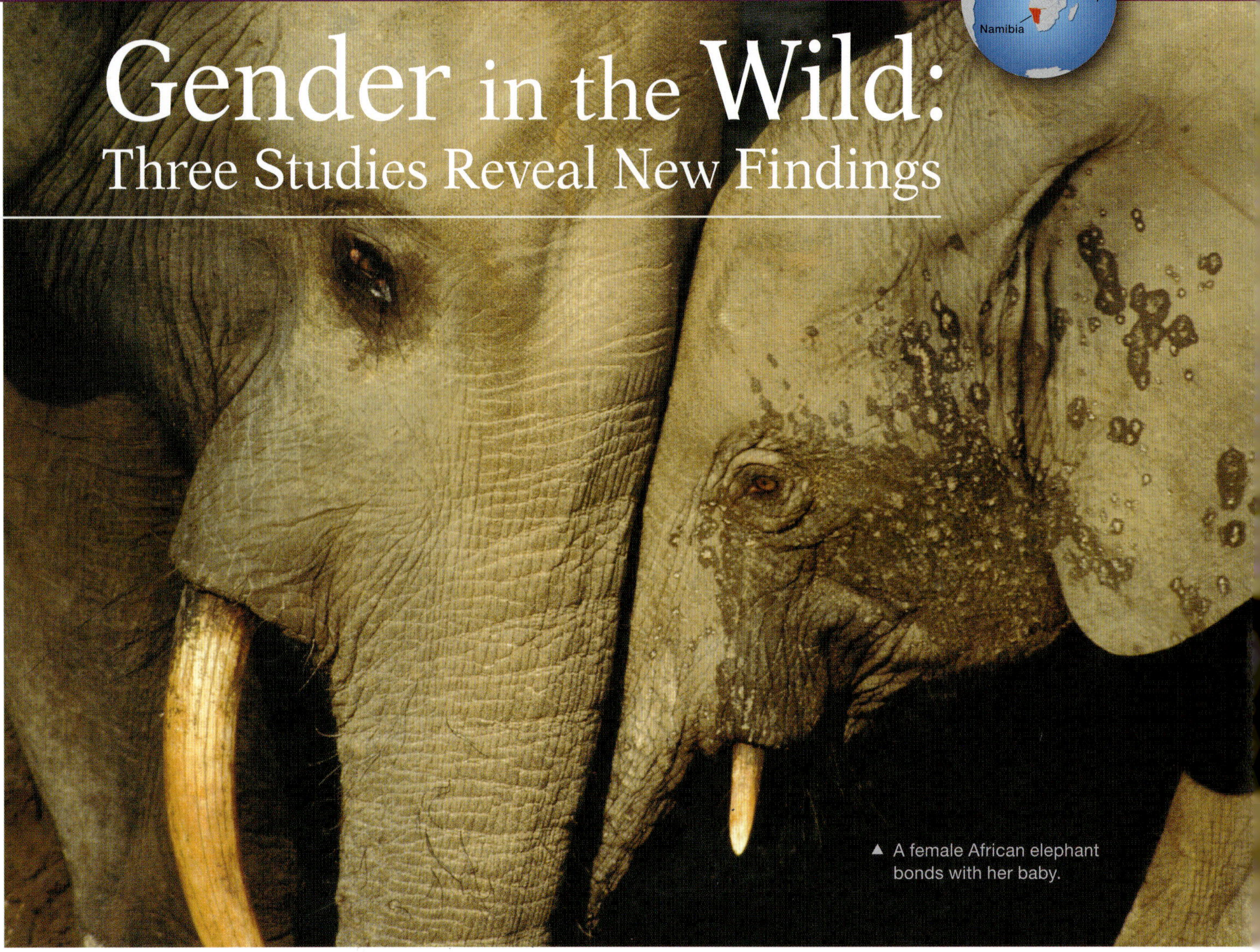

▲ A female African elephant bonds with her baby.

A How DOES GENDER impact family relationships in the wild? Studies in three African national parks reveal how gender influences the social structure of elephants, the family behavior of geladas—a species of primate—and the ways in which young chimpanzees play.

1 ETOSHA NATIONAL PARK, NAMIBIA
Studies Show Gender Effect in Elephant Societies

B Young elephants are raised within extended matriarchal[1] families.[2] Elephant mothers, aunts, grandmothers, and female friends cooperate to raise babies in large, carefully organized groups. As they grow up, young elephants look first to the birth mother for guidance and protection, and then to their female relatives and friends. This communal system[3] helps protect young orphan elephants whose mothers have been killed by hunters or farmers—in cases where elephants invade farmland due to habitat loss. When a young elephant is orphaned, other females take over the dead mother's role. The strong bonds between females continue throughout their lives, which can be as long as 70 years. In contrast, young male elephants stay close to their female family members until they are 14, and then they generally go off on their own.

C Previously, male elephants were perceived to be less social than females. However, a recent study at Etosha National Park in Namibia shows that males often form intense, long-lasting associations

▲ **Girls with power:** In gelada societies, females—like these in Simen Mountains National Park—are the real decision-makers.

2 SIMEN MOUNTAINS NATIONAL PARK, ETHIOPIA

Gelada Study Reveals Female Primates with Power

Geladas are reddish-brown-colored primates found only in the remote highlands of north-central Ethiopia. Males are larger than females and have bushy manes[5] and long tails. However, while female geladas are smaller and less distinctive-looking, they have the real power in family groups.

Since 1997, Australian wildlife biologist Chadden Hunter has been studying a group of geladas in Simen Mountains National Park in Ethiopia. Geladas live in family groups where females make the important decisions. As Hunter has observed, typical gelada family units have between two and eight adult females, their offspring, and a primary male—which researchers call the family male. Gelada males have little say in what the family does from day to day. Instead, females have the decision-making power—they decide where and how long to graze[6] for food, when to move, and where to sleep. They also choose which male will be their mate and when it is time to replace that mate with another male.

with other males. During the six-year study, Stanford University behavioral psychologist Caitlin O'Connell-Rodwell observed close, continuing bonds among a group of a dozen males. The group, which O'Connell-Rodwell named the Boys' Club, was a mix of teenagers, adults, and seniors up to age 55. Her study reveals that members of the male group follow a strict social hierarchy in which each member knows his rank or status, similar to the pecking order[4] in female extended families. Older males function as teachers and mediators (peacekeepers) for younger ones, controlling or disciplining them when conflict occurs. O'Connell-Rodwell observed that these strong bonds and rigid lines of authority are helpful during periods of drought, when food and water are scarce. "In dry years, the strict pecking order they establish benefits all of them," O'Connell-Rodwell reports. For example, the young bulls know they must get in line behind the more senior elephants. In this way, everyone gets a turn to eat and drink, conflict is avoided, and peace is maintained.

[1] In a **matriarchal** family or group, the rulers are female, and power is passed from mother to daughter.

[2] An **extended family** includes more family members than just parents and children. It also includes relatives such as aunts, uncles, cousins, and grandparents.

[3] In a **communal system**, individuals in a community share responsibilities and resources equally.

[4] A **pecking order** is the arrangement of individuals in a group according to their status or power.

[5] A **bushy mane** is the thick hair that grows around the neck of an animal such as a gelada or a lion.

[6] When animals **graze**, they eat the grass or other plants that are growing in a particular place.

SOCIAL RELATIONSHIPS | 13

LESSON B READING

Young bachelor[7] males live in separate groups. They spend most of their time observing family groups and looking for opportunities to challenge the family males. When a young bachelor comes too close to a family, the family male chases him away. To replace a family male, the females invite a bachelor to take over the family. Females typically do this when a family male becomes weak or does not give enough attention to them or their offspring. "Usually it's because the male isn't as attentive as the females want him to be," notes Hunter. "That's especially true in families where there are six or seven females; it's a lot of work to keep them all happy."

Hunter has observed that no family male lasts more than four years, and many are replaced before three. However, replaced males do not leave their families. Rather, they stay on in a kind of grandfather role. "That way, they can protect their children," he says, "and they're very aggressive about that." Hunter's study has generated new interest in geladas, and it will challenge primatologists to learn more about their gender behavior.

3 KIBALE NATIONAL PARK, UGANDA
Researchers Discover Gender-Driven Play in Chimps

Just as human boys and girls often choose different toys, some monkeys in captivity[8] have also demonstrated gender-driven toy preferences. For example, young female vervet and rhesus monkeys in captivity have been known to favor dolls, while their male counterparts prefer toys such as trucks. Now, for the first time, a study of young female chimpanzees in Kibale National Park in Uganda shows that male and female animals in the wild also play in contrasting ways.

Richard Wrangham, a primatologist at Harvard University, has been studying the play behavior of male and female chimps. His team observed that the way a community of young Kanyawara female chimps played with sticks mimicked caretaking behaviors. The young females took sticks to their nests and cared for them like mother chimps with their babies. The chimps appeared to be using the sticks as dolls, as if they were

▲ **Kibale National Park, Uganda:** Research shows that young female chimps may care for sticks like mother chimps care for their babies.

practicing for motherhood. This play preference, which was very rarely seen in males, was observed in young female chimps more than a hundred times over 14 years of study. In contrast, young males did not normally play with objects. Instead, they preferred active play—climbing, jumping, and chasing each other through trees.

Stick play may have evolved to prepare females for motherhood—giving them an evolutionary advantage by providing skills and knowledge that contribute to their survival. It is also possible that stick play is just an expression of the imagination—an ability found in chimps and humans but few other animals.

---

[7] A **bachelor** is a single male without a female partner or children.
[8] If an animal lives **in captivity**, it is kept by humans, as in a zoo.

UNDERSTANDING THE READING

A | Identifying Main Ideas. Circle the letter of the sentence that best expresses the *main* idea of each section in the reading passage.

1. **Studies Show Gender Effect in Elephant Societies**
    a. Mothers, aunts, grandmothers, and female friends usually raise elephant babies, while male elephants go off on their own.
    b. Female elephants have power in elephant families, while males form hierarchical groups with other males.

2. **Gelada Study Reveals Female Primates with Power**
    a. Females decide where to eat, when to move, and when to sleep.
    b. Female geladas control family groups in gelada society.

3. **Researchers Discover Gender-Driven Play in Chimps**
    a. The types of play that young chimps prefer seems to be related to gender.
    b. Young female chimps sometimes use sticks like human children use dolls.

B | Identifying Meaning from Context. Find the following words and expressions in the reading passage on pages 12–14. Read the words and sentences around them (the context) to decide their meanings. Complete the sentences (1–5).

| associations | bull | drought |
| have little say | in the wild | mimicked |

1. _____ elephants form social groups just as female elephants do.

2. A severe _____ can lead to the death of many animals if it kills the plants they normally eat.

3. Female elephants often form strong _____ that last for many years.

4. New employees often _____ about their projects because their managers make all the decisions about what they will work on.

5. It is easy to study animals in zoos or in laboratories, but it is difficult to study them _____.

6. Researchers noticed that a baby chimp _____ her mother when she started copying the way her mother used a stick to get food.

SOCIAL RELATIONSHIPS | 15

LESSON B
UNDERSTANDING THE READING

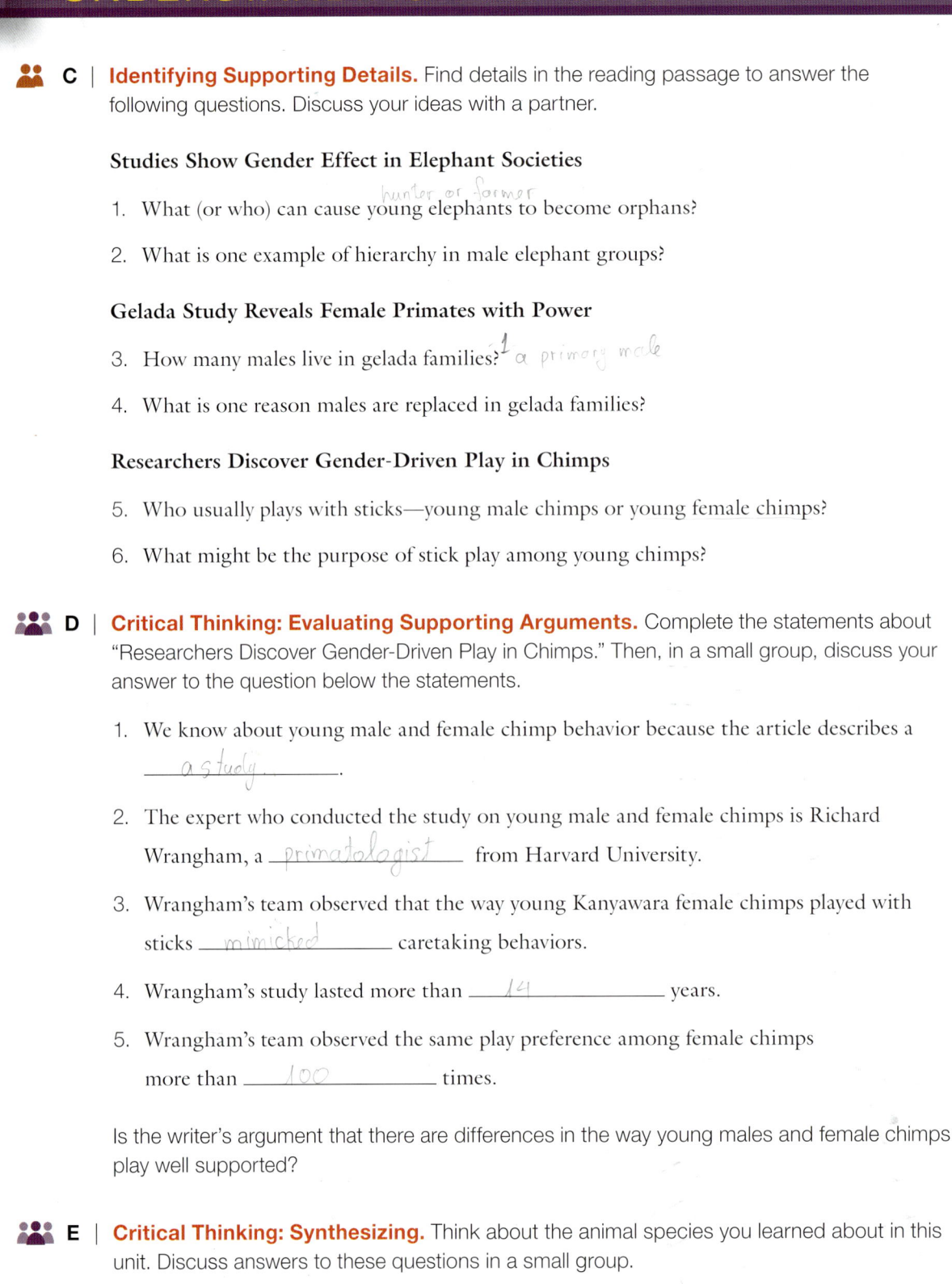

C | Identifying Supporting Details. Find details in the reading passage to answer the following questions. Discuss your ideas with a partner.

Studies Show Gender Effect in Elephant Societies

1. What (or who) can cause young elephants to become orphans? *hunter or farmer*

2. What is one example of hierarchy in male elephant groups?

Gelada Study Reveals Female Primates with Power

3. How many males live in gelada families? *1 a primary male*

4. What is one reason males are replaced in gelada families?

Researchers Discover Gender-Driven Play in Chimps

5. Who usually plays with sticks—young male chimps or young female chimps?

6. What might be the purpose of stick play among young chimps?

D | Critical Thinking: Evaluating Supporting Arguments. Complete the statements about "Researchers Discover Gender-Driven Play in Chimps." Then, in a small group, discuss your answer to the question below the statements.

1. We know about young male and female chimp behavior because the article describes a __*a study*__.

2. The expert who conducted the study on young male and female chimps is Richard Wrangham, a __*primatologist*__ from Harvard University.

3. Wrangham's team observed that the way young Kanyawara female chimps played with sticks __*mimicked*__ caretaking behaviors.

4. Wrangham's study lasted more than __*14*__ years.

5. Wrangham's team observed the same play preference among female chimps more than __*100*__ times.

Is the writer's argument that there are differences in the way young males and female chimps play well supported?

E | Critical Thinking: Synthesizing. Think about the animal species you learned about in this unit. Discuss answers to these questions in a small group.

1. In which animal societies do females have power?

2. In which animal societies is hierarchy important?

3. In which animal species is forming strong bonds important?

EXPLORING WRITTEN ENGLISH

LESSON C

GOAL: Writing about Similarities and Differences

In this lesson, you are going to plan, write, revise, and edit a paragraph on the following topic: *Think about an animal in this unit or another animal that you know about. In what ways is its behavior similar to or different from human behavior?*

A | **Brainstorming.** Choose two types of animal. Note examples of the behavior of each one.

animal 1: _____   animal 2: _____

behavior: _____   behavior: _____

_____   _____

_____   _____

Free Writing. Write for five minutes. Describe how the social behavior of one of the animals in this unit is similar to and different from a group of people you are familiar with (for example, a social group, or people in your country or culture). Use these points of comparison, or your own idea(s).

| matriarchal families | gender-based toy preferences | doing favors |
| hierarchical groups | using noises to intimidate | sharing resources |

B | Read the information in the box. Then rewrite the sentences (1–4) on page 18 with words and expressions for making comparisons.

Language for Writing: Making Comparisons

Writers use certain words and expressions to show similarities and differences between two things.

Similarities:

Office workers **are similar to** *primates. Both use conflict and cooperation in groups.*

Humans generally live in harmony. **Likewise**, *chimpanzees try to avoid conflict.*

People sometimes shout to intimidate others. **In a similar way**, *apes show aggression by pounding their chests or screeching.*

- The form of *be* in *be similar to* must agree with its subject.
- Use *likewise* and *in a similar way* at the beginning of sentences, followed by a comma.

SOCIAL RELATIONSHIPS | 17

LESSON C — EXPLORING WRITTEN ENGLISH

Language for Writing: Making Comparisons *(continued)*

Differences:

While aggression is part of normal primate behavior, it plays a limited role in the wild.

The strong bonds among females continue throughout their lives. **Conversely**, young male elephants stay close to their female family members only until they are 14. Elephant families are matriarchal. **On the other hand**, males traditionally have the power in many human cultures.

- *Conversely* and *on the other hand* can appear at the beginning of sentences, followed by a comma. They can also appear after the subject. Note the use of commas in this case: *Males,* **on the other hand**, *traditionally have the power in many human cultures.*

Example: Female geladas hold the power in the family. Males have little say about what goes on in the family. (*on the other hand*)

Female geladas hold the power in the family. On the other hand, males have little say about what goes on in the family.

1. Social networking is important in the human workplace. Chimpanzees form strong bonds within their groups. (*in a similar way*)

2. Male geladas are big and have bushy manes. Female geladas are small and less distinctive-looking. (*while*)

3. Young male chimps prefer active play. Young female chimps prefer less active play. (*conversely*)

4. Humans have invented tools to help them survive. Chimpanzees make and use tools for specific purposes. (*likewise*)

C | Applying. Rewrite your sentences from the free-writing task on page 17, using different expressions for comparison.

Writing Skill: Reviewing Paragraph Writing

A good paragraph has **one main idea**, which all the sentences in the paragraph relate to. In addition, most paragraphs include a **topic sentence** that introduces the main idea that the paragraph will discuss. Paragraphs often begin with topic sentences, but the topic sentence can appear anywhere in the paragraph.

Good paragraphs also include **supporting ideas** that give information about the main idea. To help the reader understand the main idea, writers develop their supporting ideas with **explanations** or specific **details and examples**.

In a comparison paragraph, the topic sentence tells the reader what is being compared and whether the paragraph will show differences, similarities, or both. In addition, it can mention the points of comparison. Look at this example:

Male and female geladas are different in terms of their appearance, power in their family, and caring for their young.

- groups being compared
- different/similar/both
- points of comparison

D | Critical Thinking: Analyzing. Read the paragraph below. Answer the questions and then discuss your answers with a partner.

1. What is being compared in the topic sentence?

2. Does the paragraph show differences, similarities, or both?

3. What are the three points of comparison in the paragraph?

   _____   _____   _____

4. What is one detail that supports each point of comparison?

   _____   _____   _____

   While there are some differences between monkeys and apes, these two primate groups also have some behavioral similarities. Apes are physically different from monkeys. For example, apes and monkeys have different hand structures. Apes have opposable thumbs. That is, they can use their thumbs to hold things in a similar way to humans. Monkeys, on the other hand, do not have opposable thumbs. In addition, apes are more intelligent than monkeys. For example, chimpanzees, gorillas, and bonobos have all been observed inventing and using tools, while tool use has only been observed in one species of monkey, the capuchin monkey. However, the two groups are similar in terms of cooperation. Most ape species live in communities and share resources. Likewise, most monkeys spend their lives in large groups consisting of several females and their offspring. Gelada monkeys, for example, live in groups of six to eight females, their children, and one male. In a similar way, adult chimpanzee males, females, and offspring live together in family groups. So while apes and monkeys differ in appearance and intelligence, there are similarities in the ways in which they cooperate.

LESSON C
WRITING TASK: Drafting and Revising

A | Planning. Follow the steps to make notes for your paragraph.

Step 1 Label the circle on the right side of the Venn diagram with the one of the animals you listed on page 17 (Exercise A).

Step 2 How is that animal similar to and different from humans? Think of at least two points of comparison and note similarities and differences in the diagram. Include details and examples. Don't write in complete sentences.

Step 3 Now write a topic sentence to introduce your paragraph.

Topic sentence: _____

_____

B | Draft 1. Use the notes in your Venn diagram to write a first draft of your paragraph.

C | Comparing. The paragraphs below are about two types of animals.

Which do you think is the first draft? _____   Which is the revision? _____

a While wolves are dogs' closest relatives, the two animals are different in terms of their appearance, their relationships with humans, and their social behavior. Although some dog species look similar to wolves, dogs are generally smaller than wolves and have shorter noses and smaller teeth than wolves. Dogs are friendly and have evolved to live closely with humans. In fact, dogs have been living with humans for thousands of years. For example, they helped early humans hunt. Wolves, on the other hand, are shy. They stay away from humans and usually cannot be domesticated. Wolves' social behavior is also different from that of dogs. Wolves live in family groups called packs, which can include up to 15 members. Dogs, on the other hand, do not live in family groups with other dogs. Instead, they live in human groups. Although dogs and wolves are closely related, they are different in many ways.

b While some dog species look similar to wolves, dogs are generally smaller than wolves and have shorter noses and smaller teeth than wolves. Dogs are friendly and have evolved to live closely with humans. Dogs have been living with humans for thousands of years. For example, they helped early humans hunt. Some dogs make excellent pets, but some do not. The more intelligent a dog is, the better pet it can be. Wolves do not make good pets. In fact, they frequently appear as evil characters in fairy tales. Wolves live in family groups called packs, which can include up to 15 members. Dogs, on the other hand, do not live in family groups with other dogs. Instead, they live in human groups. Although dogs and wolves are closely related, they are different in many ways.

D | Critical Thinking: Analyzing. Work with a partner. Compare the two paragraphs in Exercise **C** by answering the following questions about each one.

	a		b	
1. Is there a topic sentence?	Y	N	Y	N
2. Does the paragraph include at least two points of comparison?	Y	N	Y	N
3. Are there details and examples for each point of comparison?	Y	N	Y	N
4. Does all the information relate to the main idea?	Y	N	Y	N

Now discuss your answer to this question: Which paragraph is better? Why?

E | Revising. Answer the questions above about your own paragraph.

F | Peer Evaluation. Exchange your first draft with a partner and follow the steps below.

Step 1 Read your partner's paragraph and tell him or her one thing that you liked about it.

Step 2 Complete the Venn diagram with the similarities and/or differences that your partner describes.

Step 3 Compare your Venn diagram with the one that your partner created in exercise **A**. The two Venn diagrams should be similar. If they aren't, discuss how they differ.

LESSON C
WRITING TASK: Editing

G | Draft 2. Write a second draft of your paragraph. Use what you learned from the peer evaluation activity and your answers to exercise **E**. Make any other necessary changes.

H | Editing Practice. Read the information in the box. Then find and correct one mistake with comparison expressions in each of the sentences (1–5).

> In sentences with comparison expressions, remember:
> - that the form of *be* in *be similar to* must agree with its subject.
> - to use commas correctly in sentences with *while, likewise, in a similar way, on the other hand,* and *conversely.*

1. The use of tools among gorillas are similar to the use of tools among chimpanzees.
2. Dogs are not capable of using language. Conversely some apes are able to communicate using human sign language.
3. When greeting someone in Japan, it is the usual custom to bow. Likewise people in Korea bow when they greet others.
4. In the U.K., people drive on the left side of the road. Drivers in the U.S. on the other hand drive on the right.
5. Chimpanzee mothers and daughters form strong bonds. In a similar way adult female elephants form close relationships with young females in the family.

I | Editing Checklist. Use the checklist to find errors in your second draft.

Editing Checklist	Yes	No
1. Are all the words spelled correctly?		
2. Is the first word of every sentence capitalized?		
3. Does every sentence end with the correct punctuation?		
4. Do your subjects and verbs agree?		
5. Did you use the simple present correctly?		
6. Are verb tenses correct?		

J | Final Draft. Now use your Editing Checklist to write a third draft of your paragraph. Make any other necessary changes.

Science and Detection

UNIT 2

ACADEMIC PATHWAYS
Lesson A: Identifying a sequence of events
Distinguishing fact from speculation
Lesson B: Understanding a personal narrative/opinion article
Lesson C: Planning an opinion paragraph
Writing an opinion paragraph

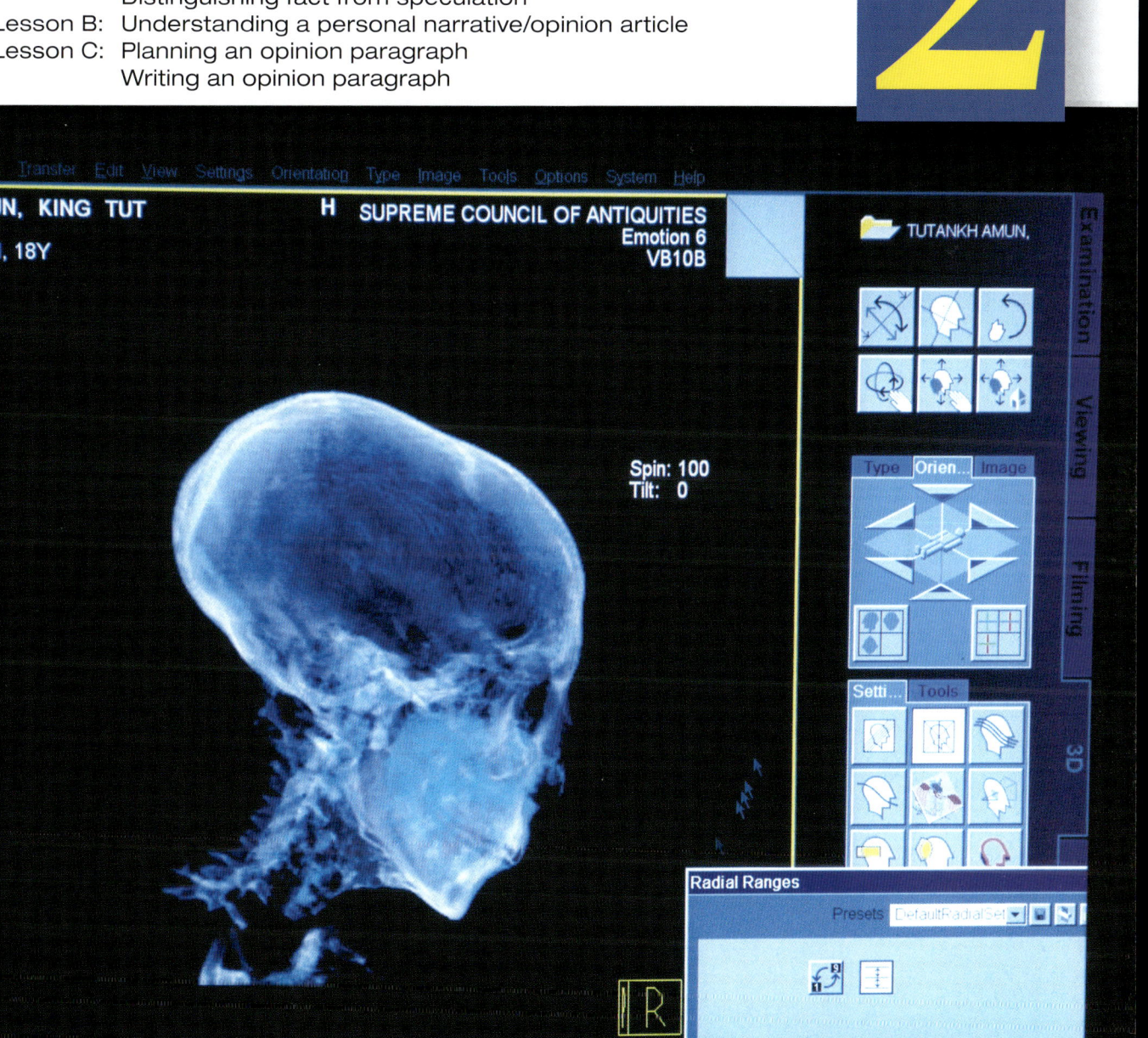

Think and Discuss

1. In what ways can science help investigators solve crimes and mysteries?
2. Do you know any historical mysteries or crime cases that were solved using technology?

▲ A CT scanner is used to investigate the cause of death of the Egyptian king Tutankhamun.

Exploring the Theme

Read the information on these pages and discuss the questions.

1. What do CT scanners do? In what ways are they used?
2. When did people start using fingerprints to identify themselves? When were fingerprints first used to solve a crime?
3. Why is DNA a useful tool for identifying people? Where can it be found?

Centuries ago, and even as recently as decades ago, there were many questions that scientists and researchers could not find the answers to. However, as technology continues to advance, identifying criminals and solving mysteries of the past is gradually becoming easier. Some mysteries, however, remain to be solved.

24 | UNIT 2

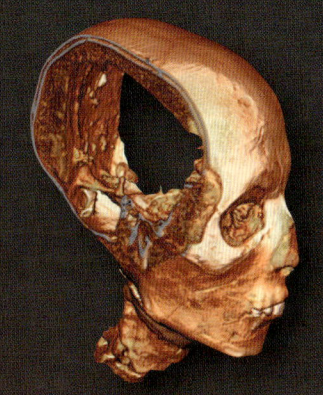

CT Scanning

A CT scanner is a medical imaging device that can take three-dimensional images of the inside of almost any object. With it, a doctor can look for tumors, infections, and internal bleeding inside a patient's body without cutting the patient open. However, CT scanners are not used solely for medical purposes. The technology can also help scientists, researchers, and detectives to investigate mysteries that are otherwise difficult to solve.

Fingerprinting

Every person on Earth has a different fingerprint pattern. Oil from fingertips can stick to almost any surface a person touches, and the oil stays in the same shape as the prints on the individual's fingers. Even if you cut or burn your fingers, the same fingerprint pattern will grow back when the injury heals. Some societies were using fingerprints as identifying markers thousands of years ago. In the second millennium BC, people pressed their fingers into clay tablets to sign contracts. These days, fingerprints are most useful for helping police solve crimes. The first crime solved by fingerprint evidence occurred in Argentina in 1892.

DNA Tracking

First discovered in 1953, DNA is a tiny molecule containing a code that gives instructions for the growth of cells in a person's body. For example, the code determines if a person will have blue eyes or brown eyes, or red hair or blond hair. DNA is found in almost every part of the body, and every individual's DNA is unique, except for the DNA of identical twins. Because each person's DNA is distinctive, it is a valuable tool for identification. Today, DNA is used to solve crimes, to identify victims of accidents, and to trace an individual's family history back hundreds or thousands of years.

◀ French paleontologist Jean-Jacques Hublin makes a CT scan of a Neanderthal skull.

SCIENCE AND DETECTION | 25

LESSON A   PREPARING TO READ

A | Building Vocabulary. Find the words and phrases in **blue** in the reading passage on pages 27–29. Use the context to guess their meanings. Then write each word or phrase below next to its definition (1–10).

| analysis | attach | commit [a crime] | deduce | detective |
| extract | identify | investigate | prime | suspect |

Word Link
The prefix **extra-** means *outside of*, e.g., **extra**ct, **extra**ordinary, **extra**curricular, **extra**terrestrial (= outside Earth)

1. _____: (verb) join or fasten something to an object
2. _____: (noun) a person who the police or authorities think may be guilty of a crime
3. _____: (adjective) the most important
4. _____: (verb) do something illegal or bad
5. _____: (noun) someone whose job is to find out what has happened in a crime
6. _____: (verb) reach a conclusion using information that you have
7. _____: (noun) the process of studying something carefully
8. _____: (verb) try to find out what happened or what is the truth
9. _____: (verb) take a substance out from something else
10. _____: (verb) name someone or something and say who or what they are

B | Using Vocabulary. Answer the questions. Share your ideas with a partner.

1. Do you think you would be good at **investigating** crimes? Why, or why not?
2. What are some ways that the police can **identify suspects**?
3. Read the following scenario. What information can you **deduce** from it?

> A man comes home from a night out with friends. He lives alone. The front door of his house is wide open. There is a shoe print on the outside of the door. He goes to the door and sees that the lock is broken. Inside, he finds that his laptop and his television are missing from the living room. His tablet computer, which was in the kitchen, is also missing. The man goes through the rest of the house and finds that nothing else is missing. However, the window in the kitchen is broken. There is blood dripping down the edges of the broken window. There is no broken glass on the kitchen floor. There is a lot of broken glass underneath the window outside the house.

C | Brainstorming. What kind of evidence do you think detectives look for when they are investigating a crime? Discuss ideas in a small group.

D | Predicting. Skim the reading passage on pages 27–29. Check (✓) the types of cases that you think will be featured. As you read, check your predictions.

☐ Plant DNA—a recent robbery   ☐ Human DNA—a recent robbery
☐ Human DNA—a recent murder   ☐ Plant DNA—a recent murder
☐ X-ray, CT scans—a prehistoric murder ☐ X-ray, CT scans—a prehistoric robbery

READING

Tech Detectives

A Police detectives have always made use of the latest technologies available to solve crimes. As three cases show, modern technology such as DNA analysis and CT¹ imaging can help scientists and detectives understand and solve mysteries both from the present and from the past.

Leech Solves Robbery² Case in Australia

B Leeches are not generally thought of as useful creatures; in fact, people usually try to avoid them. However, in 2009, detectives in Australia were able to think outside the box³ and use a leech to solve an eight-year-old robbery case. In 2001, two men robbed a 71-year-old woman in her home in the woods in Tasmania, stealing several hundred dollars. The men escaped, but, soon after, detectives investigating the crime scene found a leech filled with blood.

C The detectives speculated that the leech could have attached itself to one of the robbers, sucked his blood while he was traveling through the woods, and then fallen off during the robbery. The detectives extracted some DNA from the blood in the leech and kept it in their database.⁴

Eight years later, police arrested a suspect on an unrelated drug charge. As part of his examination, his DNA was analyzed, and it soon turned out to match that taken from the leech. After being questionned by the police, the suspect eventually admitted to committing the 2001 robbery.

---

¹ **CT** stands for Computer Tomography.
² A **robbery** is the crime of stealing money or property, often using force.
³ When you **think outside the box**, you think creatively and come up with new and unusual ideas.
⁴ A **database** is a collection of data, or information, that is stored in a computer and can easily be accessed.

SCIENCE AND DETECTION | 27

LESSON A READING

▲ Flowers of the palo verde tree

Plant Helps Solve Murder Case in Arizona

The first conviction[5] based on plant DNA evidence occurred in the state of Arizona, in the United States. When a murder was committed in 1992 in the state capital, Phoenix, a pager[6] found at the scene of the crime led the police to a prime suspect. The suspect admitted to giving the victim a ride in his truck, but denied any wrongdoing. In fact, he claimed that she had actually robbed him, thus explaining how his pager had been found at the crime scene. Forensic investigators examined his truck and found seed pods, which were later identified as the fruits of the palo verde tree. And indeed, a palo verde tree at the scene of the crime showed signs of having been hit by a truck.

However, this evidence alone was not enough. So an investigator wondered if it was possible to link the exact tree at the crime scene with the seed pods found on the truck. A geneticist at the University of Arizona in Tucson demonstrated that it was; individual plants—in this case palo verde trees—have unique patterns of DNA. Analysis proved that the truck had definitely been to the crime scene and had collided with one specific tree, contradicting the suspect's story. With this information, it was possible to convict the suspect of the crime.

Who Killed the Iceman?

Europe's oldest mummy,[7] now known as the Iceman, was discovered by hikers in the frozen ice of the Italian Alps in 1991. Scientists believe he lived about 5,300 years ago in an area north of what is now Bolzano, Italy. Wounds on the Iceman's body have made it clear to scientists for some time that he died a violent death. But new DNA analysis, along with X-ray and CT imaging technology, has helped scientists piece together even more clues about the life and death of this ancient Neolithic[8] human.

CT imaging identified an arrowhead buried in the Iceman's left shoulder, indicating that he was shot from behind. Scientists also found a wound on one of his hands, leading them to believe that he had been in a fight with one or more enemies who later chased after and killed him. While this may be the case, close analysis of this hand injury shows that the wound was already beginning to close and heal at the time of his death. So it is unlikely he sustained it in his final days. Moreover, a later study of the CT images revealed that the Iceman had a full stomach at the time he was killed. This meant that he ate a big meal immediately before his death—not something a person being chased by enemies would do. Scientists deduced that the Iceman was probably resting after a meal and was attacked from behind.

Perhaps the most likely theory is that the Iceman was fleeing an earlier battle, but thought he was safe at the moment of his murder. Scientists continue to analyze the Iceman using the latest technology to find more clues to history's oldest murder mystery.

---

[5] If someone has a **conviction**, they are found guilty of a crime in a court of law.
[6] A **pager** is an electronic device that is used for contacting someone.
[7] A **mummy** is a dead body that was preserved long ago, usually by being rubbed with special oils and wrapped in cloth.
[8] If something is **Neolithic**, it is from the last part of the Stone Age, a period that occurred between 9000 and 6000 BC in Asia, and between 4000 and 2400 BC in Europe.

An artist's view of the ▶ Iceman's final moments: An arrowhead discovered in the Iceman's left shoulder indicates that he was shot from behind and was probably unaware of his killers.

SCIENCE AND DETECTION | 29

LESSON A — UNDERSTANDING THE READING

A | Identifying Main Ideas. Which technologies were used in each investigation? Check (✓) the correct columns in the chart below for items 1–3.

	Leech Solves Robbery Case in Australia	Plant Helps Solve Murder Case in Arizona	Who Killed the Iceman?
1. X-rays			✓
2. CT imaging			✓
3. DNA	✓	✓	✓
4. What evidence gave investigators useful information about the crime?	a _leech_ filled with _blood_	_seed pods_ from a palo verde tree	_arrowhead_ in the Iceman's shoulder; a full _stomach_

B | Identifying Key Details. What evidence was useful to investigators? Complete item 4 in the chart above with information from the reading passage.

> **CT Focus:** Distinguishing Fact from Speculation
>
> A **speculation** is an opinion or a guess based on incomplete information. To **distinguish fact from speculation**, look for key words. These words usually indicate a fact: *absolutely, clear, definitely, discover, know, prove, show*. These words usually indicate a speculation: *argue, believe, could, may, might, claim, likely/unlikely, opinion, perhaps, probably, speculate, theory*.

C | Critical Thinking: Distinguishing Fact from Speculation. Read these statements about the reading passage. Write **F** for *fact* or **S** for *speculation* next to each one. Circle the words that support your answers.

1. __S__ The detectives (speculated) that the leech (could have) attached itself to one of the robbers.

2. __F__ Analysis proved that the truck had definitely been to the crime scene.

3. __S__ Perhaps the most likely theory is that the Iceman was fleeing an earlier battle, but thought he was safe at the moment of his murder.

4. __F__ Wounds on the Iceman's body have made it clear he died a violent death.

5. __S__ It is unlikely he sustained [the wound] in his final days.

D | Speculating. What do investigators think probably happened to the Iceman? Do you agree? Can you think of other interpretations of the evidence? Discuss your answers with a partner.

DEVELOPING READING SKILLS

Reading Skill: Identifying a Sequence of Events

A crime must happen before detectives can investigate and find evidence. When you are trying to understand the sequence of events in a mystery or detective story, think about two time periods: the sequence of events *at the time of* the crime and the sequence of events *after* the crime.

Look for certain words and phrases in the story to help you understand the sequence, or order, of events.

Time markers such as days, months, years, and times of day:
on Monday   **in March**   **in 1991**   **at 5:30**

Words that indicate that one event happened before another event:
before   **earlier**   **(one year) ago**   **already**

Words that indicate that one event happened after another event:
later   **after**   **now**   **once**   **new**

Words and phrases that indicate that two events occurred at the same time:
at the time of   **at that moment**   **at the same time**   **while**

Words and phrases that indicate that something happened much earlier:
a long time ago   **for some time**   **in ancient (times)**   **in prehistoric (times)**

A | Analyzing. Read the information about the Iceman. Underline the words and phrases that show order. Then number the events in the order that they occurred.

- ☐ Europe's oldest mummy, now known as the Iceman, was discovered by hikers in the frozen ice of the Italian Alps in 1991.

- ☐ Scientists believe he lived about 5,300 years ago in an area north of what is now Bolzano, Italy.

- ☐ New DNA analysis, along with X-ray and CT imaging technology, has helped scientists piece together even more clues about the life and death of this ancient Neolithic human.

B | Applying. Reread the story "Leech Solves Robbery Case in Australia." Number the events in the order that they occurred. Think about both the sequence of events at the time of the crime and after the crime.

a. __9__ The suspect admitted that he committed the robbery.

b. __6__ Police arrested a suspect on a drug charge.

c. __7__ Police analyzed the drug charge suspect's DNA.

d. __2__ Two men entered a house to rob the woman who lived there.

e. __3__ The leech fell off of the robber.

f. __1__ A leech sucked blood from a robber.

g. __4__ Detectives found a leech filled with blood in the house.

h. __5__ Detectives took blood out of the leech.

i. __8__ Detectives matched the DNA from the leech with the DNA of the suspect.

VIEWING

Columbus DNA

Are the remains of Christopher Columbus buried in a cathedral in Seville, Spain (right), or in the Cathedral of Santa Maria in Domincan Republic (left)? Scientists hope to solve the mystery with the help of DNA.

Before Viewing

A | Using a Dictionary. Here are some words and expressions you will hear in the video. Match each word or expression with the correct definition. Use your dictionary to help you.

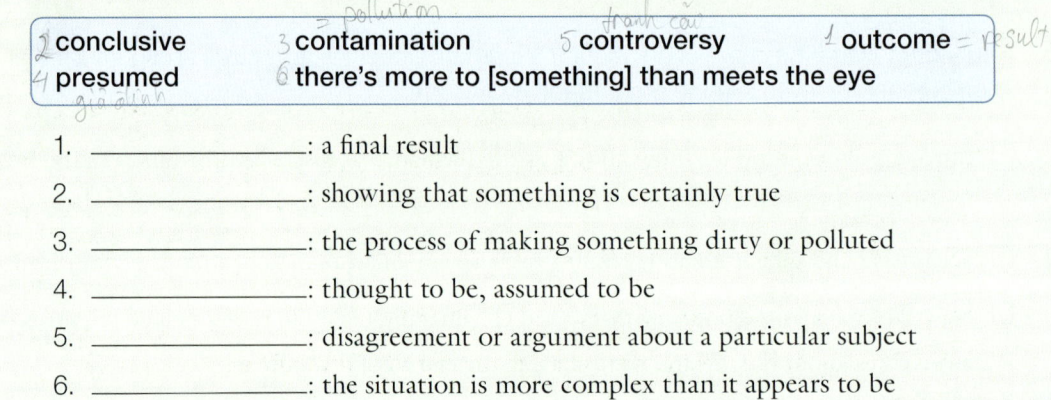

conclusive	contamination	controversy	outcome
presumed	there's more to [something] than meets the eye		

1. _____: a final result
2. _____: showing that something is certainly true
3. _____: the process of making something dirty or polluted
4. _____: thought to be, assumed to be
5. _____: disagreement or argument about a particular subject
6. _____: the situation is more complex than it appears to be

B | Thinking Ahead. What do you know about Christopher Columbus? What do you already know about DNA? Discuss with a partner.

While Viewing

Read questions 1–4. Think about the answers as you view the video.

1. Why were Columbus's remains moved to Hispaniola after he was originally buried in Spain?
2. What happened to his remains in 1795?
3. Why is there controversy about where Columbus is buried?
4. Whose bones are scientists studying in order to determine where Columbus is buried?

After Viewing

A | Discuss your answers to questions 1–4 above with a partner.

B | Critical Thinking: Synthesizing. Think about the stories in "Tech Detectives" and the video. How has technology allowed us to discover things that we could not know before?

PREPARING TO READ

LESSON B

A | Building Vocabulary. Find the words in **blue** in the reading passage on pages 34–38. Use the context to guess their meanings. Then write the correct word from the box to complete each sentence (1–10).

| comprises 4 | conduct 9 | consequence 10 | examination 6 | identity 7 |
| infectious 3 | obtain 8 | sample 1 | scholar 2 | vulnerable 5 |

1. A(n) _____ of a substance is a small amount of it that is studied and analyzed.
2. A(n) _____ is a person who studies an academic subject and knows a lot about it.
3. You can get a(n) _____ disease by being near a person who has it.
4. If something _____ a number of things or people, it includes or contains them.
5. Someone who is _____ is weak and without protection, and can be easily hurt physically or emotionally.
6. A(n) _____ of something is a close study of it.
7. Your _____ is who you are.
8. To _____ something is to get it.
9. If you _____ an investigation or an activity, you organize it and do it.
10. A(n) _____ of something is a result or an effect of it.

> **Word Link**
> com-/con- = together, with: **com**prise, **com**bine, **com**pact, **com**panion, **con**ceive, **con**duct, **con**sequence, **con**sensus, **con**struct

B | Using Vocabulary. Discuss these questions with a partner.

1. What are some possible **consequences** of committing a crime?
2. What are some things that can make a person **vulnerable** to illness?
3. What kinds of things can a person show or do to prove his or her **identity**?

C | Brainstorming. What do you already know about Egyptian pharaohs and King Tutankhamun? List ideas in a small group.

_____
_____

D | Predicting. Read the title and the headings in the reading passage on pages 34–38 and answer the question. As you read, check your prediction

What major mysteries does the passage investigate?

a. what the pharaoh's political career was like
b. what caused the pharaoh's death
c. who the pharaoh's family members were

SCIENCE AND DETECTION | **33**

King Tut's Family Secrets

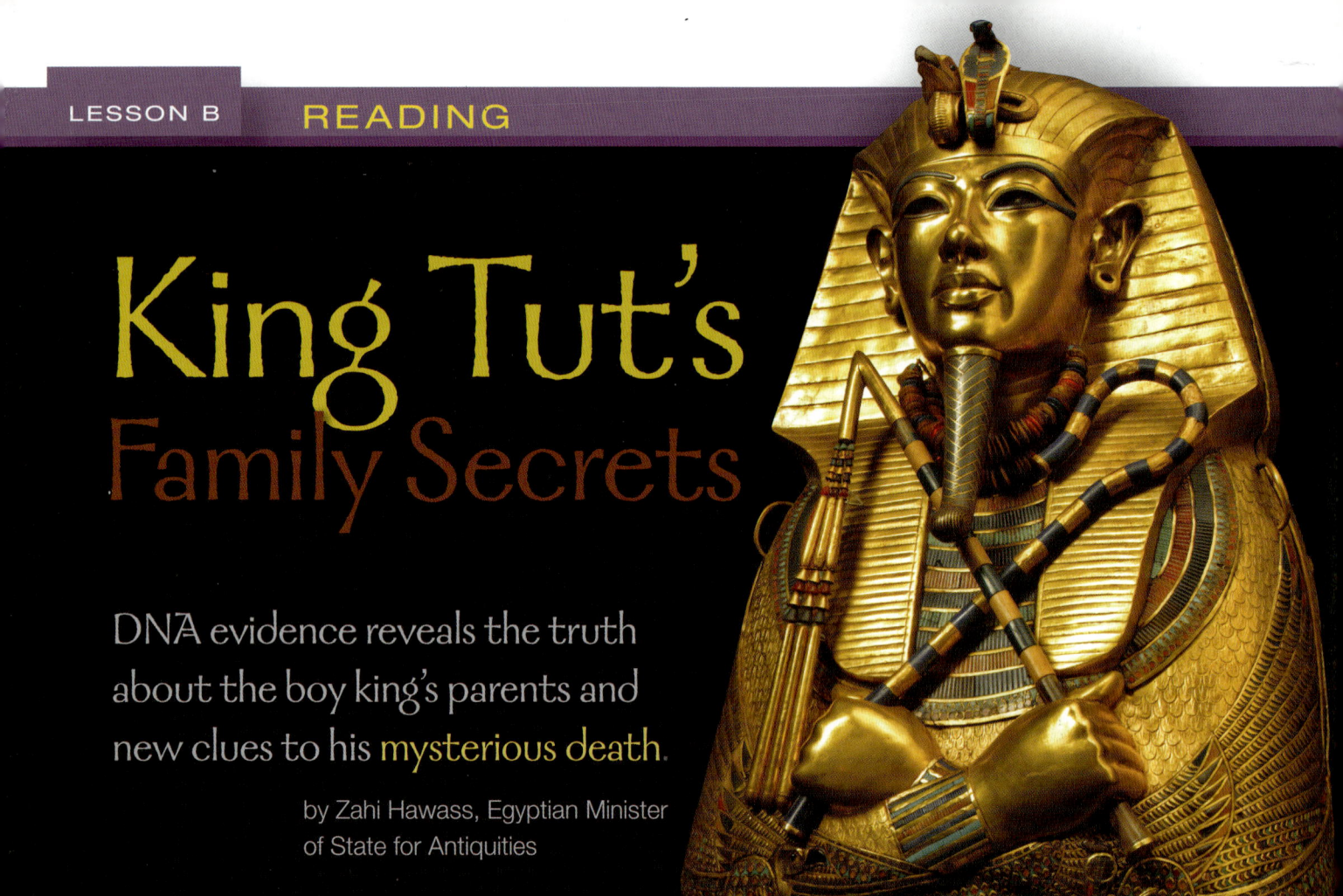

DNA evidence reveals the truth about the boy king's parents and new clues to his **mysterious death**.

by Zahi Hawass, Egyptian Minister of State for Antiquities

As an archaeologist and scholar of ancient Egyptian history, I have conflicting feelings about conducting scientific research on mummies. On the one hand, I believe that we should honor these ancient dead and let them rest in peace. On the other hand, there are some secrets of the ancient Egyptian kings, or pharaohs, that we can learn only by studying their mummies. Let me use the example of King Tutankhamun to illustrate what I mean.

Unlocking a Mystery

When Tutankhamun died about 3,000 years ago, he was secretly buried in a small tomb in a desert area near what is now the city of Luxor. When the tomb was rediscovered in 1922, the king's treasures—more than 5,000 artifacts[1]—were still inside. Among the artifacts was the pharaoh's solid gold coffin holding his mummified remains. There was a gold mask of the king and a golden fan showing him riding a chariot and hunting birds. There were also 130 staffs, or walking sticks. Mysteriously, there were also two mummified fetuses[2] found in the tomb. Another mystery: an examination of Tutankhamun's mummy revealed a hole in the back of his skull. Could it be related to the cause of his death?

These mummies and artifacts were an extremely important archaeological discovery, but they did not answer many questions about the young pharaoh and his family. How did he die? Who were his mother and father and his wife? Were the two mummified fetuses his unborn children? To solve these mysteries required further study and the use of modern technology.

CT Scans and DNA Analysis

In 2005, my colleagues and I carried out CT scans[3] of Tutankhamun's mummy. We were able to show that the hole in Tutankhamun's skull was not the cause of his death, but was made during the

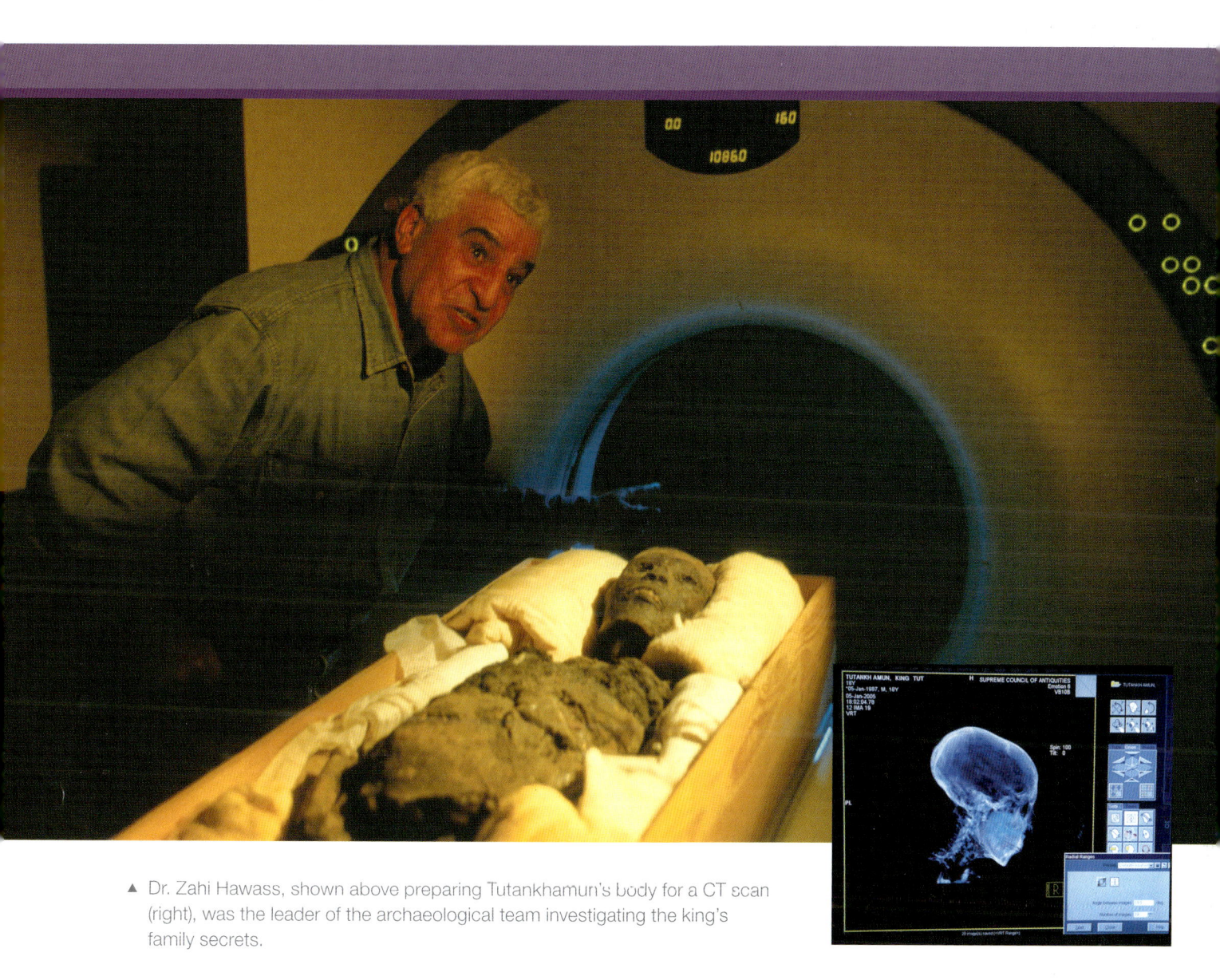

▲ Dr. Zahi Hawass, shown above preparing Tutankhamun's body for a CT scan (right), was the leader of the archaeological team investigating the king's family secrets.

mummification process. Our study also showed that Tutankhamun died when he was only 19, soon after fracturing his left leg. However, the CT scans alone could not solve the mystery of how the king died, or why he died so young.

In 2008, my colleagues and I decided to analyze samples of Tutankhamun's DNA extracted from bone tissue of his mummy. Early in the study, our team made some new discoveries: Tutankhamun's left foot was clubbed,[4] one toe was missing a bone, and bones in part of the foot were destroyed by a condition known as necrosis, or tissue death. The club foot and bone disease would have made it difficult for the young king to walk. The discovery shone light on why so many staffs had been found in Tutankhamun's tomb. Some scholars had argued that the staffs were symbols of power. Our DNA study showed that the king did not just carry staffs as symbols of power. He also needed them to walk.

Our team also tested Tutankhamun's mummy for evidence of infectious diseases. We found the presence of DNA from a parasite[5] called *Plasmodium falciparum*, which meant that Tutankhamun suffered from malaria. Did malaria kill the king? Perhaps. Its most serious forms can lead to death. My opinion, however, is that Tutankhamun's health was endangered the moment he was born. To explain what I mean, let me describe our study of Tutankhamun's royal family.

---

[1] An **artifact** is an ornament, a tool, or other object that is made by a human being, especially one that is culturally or historically interesting.

[2] A **fetus** is an animal or a human being in its later stages of development before it is born.

[3] A **CT scan**, or CAT scan, is an image that can show cross-section views of the inside of a person's body.

[4] When a foot is **clubbed**, it is deformed so that the foot is twisted inward and most of the person's weight rests on the heel.

[5] A **parasite** is a small animal or plant that lives on or inside a larger animal or plant.

SCIENCE AND DETECTION | 35

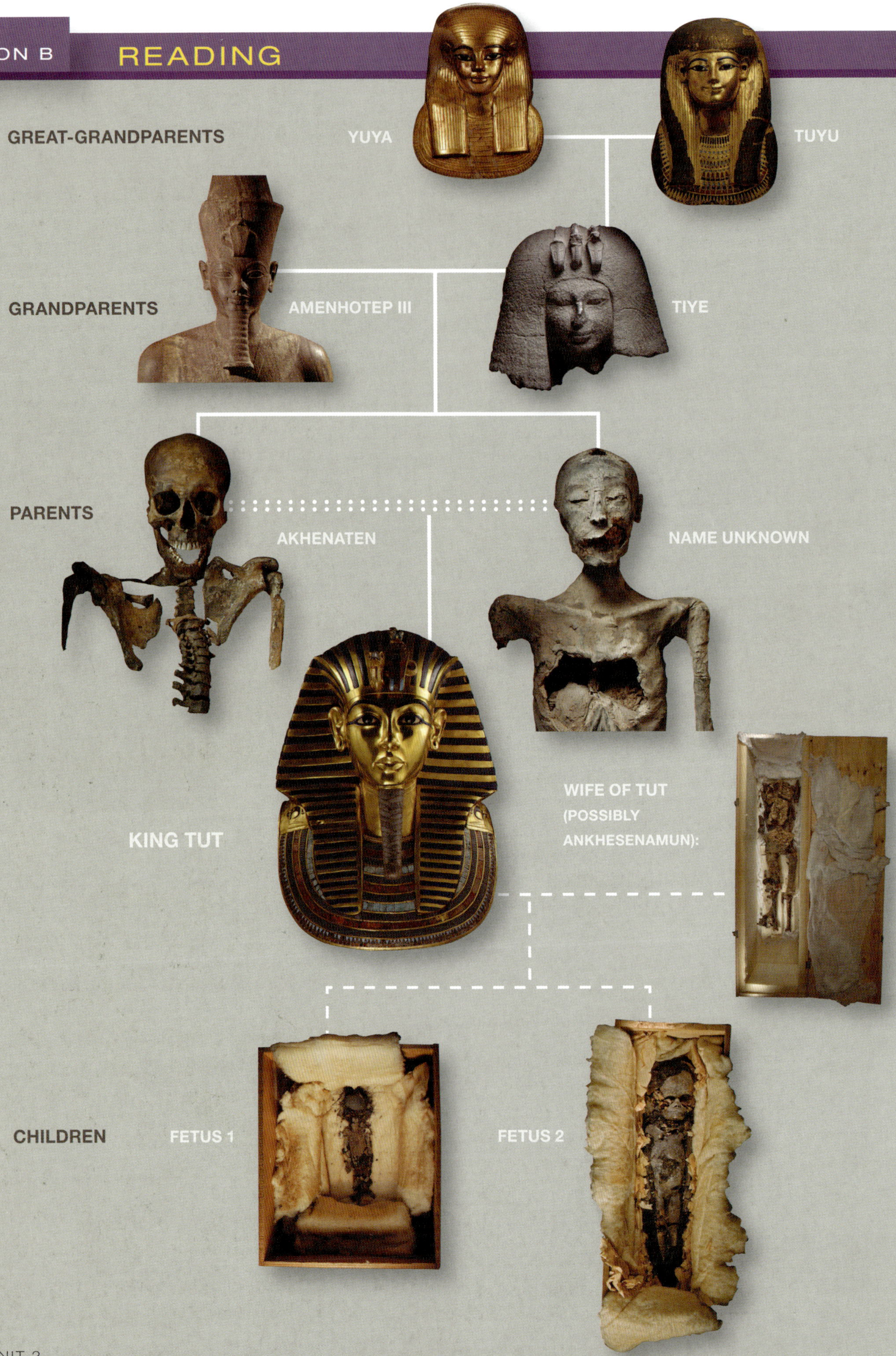

LESSON B READING

GREAT-GRANDPARENTS YUYA TUYU

GRANDPARENTS AMENHOTEP III TIYE

PARENTS AKHENATEN NAME UNKNOWN

KING TUT WIFE OF TUT (POSSIBLY ANKHESENAMUN)

CHILDREN FETUS 1 FETUS 2

36 | UNIT 2

Tracing Tut's Family Tree

Our team analyzed Tutankhamun's DNA and that of ten other mummies we believed were members of his royal family. We knew the identities of three members of his family—Amenhotep III as well as Yuya and Tuyu (the parents of Amenhotep III's wife, Tiye). The other seven mummies were unknown. They comprised an adult male and four adult females found in tombs near Tutankhamun's, and the two fetuses in Tutankhamun's tomb.

We first obtained DNA samples from the male mummies to solve the mystery of Tutankhamun's father. Many scholars believed his father was the pharaoh Akhenaten, but the archaeological evidence was unclear. Through a combination of CT scans and a comparison of DNA, our team was able to identify Amenhotep III and Tiye, one of the unidentified female mummies, as the grandparents of Tutankhamun. Moreover, our study revealed that the unidentified male adult mummy was almost certainly Akhenaten, a son of Amenhotep III and Tiye. This supported the theory that Akhenaten was Tutankhamun's father.

What about Tutankhamun's mother? We discovered that the DNA of one of the unidentified female mummies matched that of the young king. To our surprise, her DNA proved that, like Akhenaten, she was a child of Amenhotep III and Tiye. This meant that Akhenaten's wife was his own sister—and Tutankhamun was their son.

How Did Tut Die?

As I mentioned earlier, I believe that Tutankhamun's health was compromised[6] from birth. As our study showed, his mother and father were brother and sister. Such a relationship was not uncommon among royal families in ancient Egypt, as it offered political advantages. However, it also had dangerous consequences. Married siblings are more likely to pass on harmful genes, leaving their children vulnerable to a variety of genetic defects.[7] Tutankhamun's clubbed foot and bone disease may therefore have been genetic conditions. These problems, together with an attack of severe malaria or a leg broken in an accident, may have combined to cause the king's premature[8] death.

While the data are still incomplete, our study also suggests that one of the mummified fetuses is Tutankhamun's daughter and that the other may also be his child. We have only partial data from the two other unidentified female mummies. One of these may be the mother of the infant mummies and Tutankhamun's wife, possibly a woman named Ankhesenamun. We know from history that she was the daughter of Akhenaten and his wife, Nefertiti, and therefore probably was Tutankhamun's half sister. The two unborn children may have been the result of another genetic defect, one which did not allow Tutankhamun and Ankhesenamun to conceive a living heir.[9]

---

[6] If someone's health is **compromised**, it is weakened.
[7] **Genetic defects** are health problems that are inherited, or passed down, through a family line.
[8] Something that is **premature** happens earlier than people expect.
[9] An **heir** is someone who has the right to inherit a person's money, property, or title when that person dies.

▲ King Tut pictured with his wife, in a scene from the pharoah's golden throne.

LESSON B   READING

An End... and a New Beginning

After Tutankhamun's death, a new pharaoh, Ramses I, came to power, marking the start of a new dynasty.[10] Under his grandson, Ramses the Great, Egypt rose to new heights of imperial power. As their power grew, the rulers of this new dynasty tried to erase all records of Tutankhamun and his royal family from history. Through ongoing DNA research, our team seeks to honor the members of Tutankhamun's family and keep their memories alive.

[10] A **dynasty** is a series of rulers of a country who all belong to the same family.

Tutankhamun's treasures, including this decorated collar (below) and golden mask (above), continue to draw crowds of tourists to the Egyptian Museum in Cairo.

UNDERSTANDING THE READING

A | Identifying Main Ideas. Write the paragraph letter for each of these main ideas from the reading.

1. __F__ Hawass and his team studied King Tut's DNA and found out that he had a bone disease.
2. __J__ King Tut's health may have been weakened because his parents were brother and sister.
3. __C__ Hawass decided to use technology to answer some questions remaining from the discovery of King Tut's tomb.
4. __H__ Hawass and his team used DNA samples to try to determine who King Tut's father was.
5. __A__ Hawass has conflicting feelings about studying mummies.
6. __E__ Hawass's analysis of King Tut's DNA revealed that he had suffered from malaria.

B | Identifying Meaning from Context. Find and underline the following words in the reading passage on pages 34–38. Use context to help you identify the part of speech and meaning of each word. Write your answers, and then check your ideas in a dictionary.

1. honor (paragraph A)   Part of speech: _____
   Meaning: _to respect_
2. illustrate (paragraph A)   Part of speech: _____
   Meaning: _to give an example_
3. tomb (paragraph B)   Part of speech: _____
   Meaning: _where burying the dead (a burial place)_
4. staffs (paragraph B)   Part of speech: _____
   Meaning: _walking stick_
5. mummification (paragraph D) Part of speech: _to mummify_
   Meaning: _to mummify_
6. fracturing (paragraph D)   Part of speech: _____
   Meaning: _crack_
7. siblings (paragraph J)   Part of speech: _____
   Meaning: _people were born by same parents; sister, brother_

C | Identifying Supporting Details. Find details in the reading passage and the photos to answer the following questions.

1. Who were Tutankhamun's parents? _Akhenaten & his own sister (son & daughter of Amenhotep III & Tiye)_
2. Who might have been Tutankhamun's wife? _Ankhesenamun — His sister (half sister)_
3. According to the reading, what is one possible reason why Tutankhamun and his wife did not have any living children? _b/c of another genetic defect_
4. What are two medical problems that Tutankhamun had? _1. left foot was clubbed — bone disease 2. suffered from malaria_

LESSON B | UNDERSTANDING THE READING

5. Hawass believes that Tutankhamun's health was weak from the moment he was born. Why does he think so? _b/c his parent were brother & sister_

D | Identifying a Sequence of Events. Number these events in the order that they occurred. Look for words and phrases in the reading that show sequence of events. Think about both the time period when King Tut lived and the time of Hawass's team's research.

1. _6_ Hawass and his team discovered that Tutankhamun had a club foot and bone disease.
2. _4_ Hawass and his team decided to study DNA from Tutankhamun's mummy.
3. _3_ Tutankhamun's tomb was rediscovered.
4. _2_ A hole was made in Tutankhamun's skull.
5. _1_ Tutankhamun died.
6. _7_ Hawass and his team extracted DNA from the male mummies in the tomb.
7. _5_ Hawass and his team made CT scans of Tutankhamun's mummy.
8. _8_ Hawass and his team studied DNA from one of the female mummies in the tomb.

E | Critical Thinking: Distinguishing Fact from Speculation. Read these statements about the reading. Write **F** for *fact* or **S** for *speculation* next to each one. Circle the words that support your answers.

1. _F_ When the tomb was rediscovered in 1922, the king's treasures—more than 5,000 artifacts—were still inside.
2. _F_ We were able to show that the hole in Tutankhamun's skull was not the cause of his death.
3. _F_ Early in the study, our team made a new discovery—bones in part of the foot were destroyed by a condition known as necrosis.
4. _S_ Did malaria kill the king? Perhaps.
5. _S_ My opinion is that Tutankhamun's health was endangered the moment he was born.
6. _F_ To our surprise, the unidentified female mummy's DNA proved that, like Akhenaten, she was a child of Amenhotep III and Tiye.
7. _S_ Tutankhamun's clubbed foot and bone disease may have been genetic conditions.
8. _S_ One of these mummies may be the mother of the infant mummies and Tutankhamun's wife, possibly a woman named Ankhesenamun.

F | Critical Thinking: Synthesizing. Discuss answers to these questions in a small group.

1. What technologies were mentioned in both reading passages in this unit?
2. How is Hawass's team's examination of Tutankhamun similar to scientists' examination of the Iceman? How are the investigations different?

G | Critical Thinking: Inferring Attitude. Discuss answers to these questions in a small group.

1. Why does Hawass have "conflicting feelings" about studying mummies?
2. Why do you think he decided to study the mummies in Tutankhamun's tomb?

EXPLORING WRITTEN ENGLISH

LESSON C

GOAL: Writing an Opinion Paragraph
In this lesson, you are going to plan, write, revise, and edit a paragraph on the following topic: **Should scientists conduct scientific research on mummies?**

A | **Brainstorming.** Reread the first paragraph of the reading on page 34. Think of some reasons why scientists *should* and *should not* conduct scientific research on mummies. List your ideas in the chart.

Reasons Why Scientists Should Conduct Research on Mummies	Reasons Why Scientists Should Not Conduct Research on Mummies
to understand how they died	to honor the dead

Free Writing. Look at your brainstorming notes and decide whether you feel scientists should or should not conduct research on mummies. Choose one or two ideas from your notes and write for five minutes. Develop your arguments to support your opinion.

B | Read the information in the box below. Then complete the paragraph on page 42 with modals of obligation and possibility.

Language for Writing: Review of Modals of Obligation and Possibility

When writers express an opinion, they sometimes use the modal *should* to talk about an **obligation**, or the best thing to do.

> On the one hand, I believe that we **should** honor these ancient dead people and let them rest in peace.

Writers may also use the modals of **possibility** *might* and *could* to support their reasons by showing the potential results of the action they recommend. Note that *could* is also the past tense form of *can*.

> We **could** learn more about the prehistoric world if scientists received government funds to conduct further studies of the Iceman.

Remember that modals are followed by the base form of a verb.

SCIENCE AND DETECTION | 41

LESSON C | EXPLORING WRITTEN ENGLISH

Many people believe that all crime suspects _____ give DNA samples to the police. Moreover, some governments want to pass laws requiring all possible suspects to provide DNA samples. I believe that people _____ not be required to give samples of their DNA in these situations. First, there is the possibility that a technician _____ misread a DNA sample in the laboratory. For example, if the technician is tired, he _____ state that there is an 80 percent match between the suspect's DNA and the DNA found at a crime scene when in fact there is only an 8 percent match. Because the person is a possible suspect, saying the match is 80 percent accurate _____ lead police to believe that the person committed the crime. This mistake _____ lead to the conviction of an innocent person—that is, a person who did not commit the crime. The other reason I believe governments _____ not require DNA samples from suspects is that the person _____ have simply been at the crime location by chance. However, the existence of an innocent person's DNA at the crime scene _____ lead to a conviction.

C | Applying. Write 3–4 sentences giving your opinion on the issue discussed above: Should all crime suspects have to give DNA samples to the police? Give reasons for your opinion.

Writing Skill: Planning an Opinion Paragraph

When you are giving your opinion about a topic in a paragraph, be sure to include the following three elements:

A topic sentence: a sentence that clearly states your opinion on the topic (This is often—but not always—the first sentence of the paragraph.)

Supporting ideas: sentences that give reasons for your opinion

Details: examples that support your reasons (The expressions *for example,* or *for instance* are often used to give details.)

(See Unit 1 page 19 for more on paragraph writing.)

D | Identifying Parts of an Opinion Paragraph. In the paragraph above from exercise **B**, circle the topic sentence and underline the supporting ideas. Check (✓) the sentence(s) with a detail or an example.

E | Critical Thinking: Analyzing. The sentences below belong in one paragraph about eyewitness accounts. Eyewitness accounts are reports given in court by people who witnessed, or saw, a crime occur. Read the sentences and, for each one, write **T** for *topic sentence*, **S** for *supporting idea or reason*, or **D** for *detail* or example.

_____ a. I do not believe that eyewitness accounts should be used in trials.

_____ b. For instance, our memory might change when we receive additional information about an event we experienced in the past.

_____ c. Another reason is that witnesses sometimes believe that if the police think a suspect committed a crime, that person must be guilty.

_____ d. One reason is that research shows we do not always remember things exactly the way they actually happened.

_____ e. Eyewitnesses might assume the police have other evidence against the suspect, and so they might believe they saw the suspect at the crime scene.

F | Now use the sentences from exercise **E** to write a paragraph.

_____
_____
_____
_____
_____
_____
_____
_____
_____
_____
_____
_____

LESSON C
WRITING TASK: Drafting and Revising

A | Planning. Follow the steps to make notes for your paragraph.

Step 1 Think about this question: Should scientists conduct scientific research on mummies? Write your opinion in the center of the idea map. Your opinion will be the main idea of your paragraph.

Step 2 Decide the two best supporting ideas that give information about your opinion. Note these ideas in the idea map.

Step 3 Think of two details that explain each supporting idea. Note these details in the idea map.

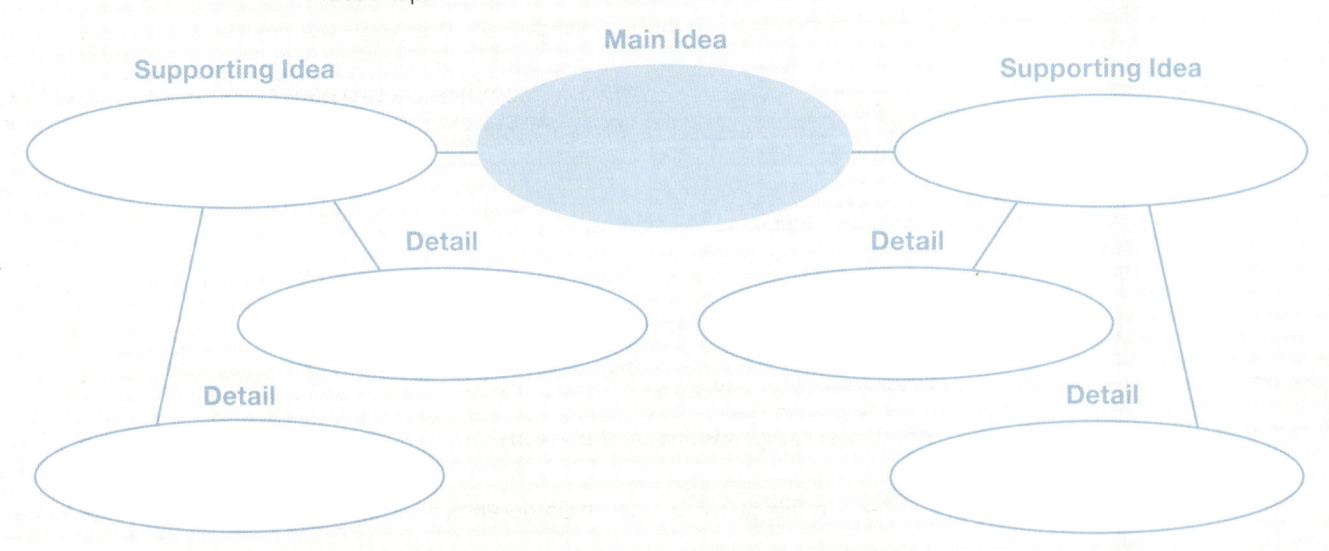

[Idea map with Main Idea in center, two Supporting Ideas branching out, each with a Detail, and two additional Detail bubbles]

B | Draft 1. Use your idea map to write a first draft of your paragraph on the topic: *Should scientists conduct scientific research on mummies?*

C | Revising. The following paragraphs **a** and **b** express an opinion about national DNA databanks.
(DNA databanks are collections of DNA information about all of the individuals in a country.) Some people think governments should require everyone to provide their DNA. Others think this is a bad idea.

Which is the first draft? _____   Which is the revision? _____

a   In my opinion, people should be required to give DNA samples to be kept in a national databank. First of all, it would save time and money. Currently in many countries, people cannot be forced to provide a DNA sample, even if they are accused of a crime. With a DNA databank, police might be able to identify criminals more quickly and easily if they had access to everyone's DNA information. Investigations could take less time and fewer resources, and this would save the government and taxpayers money. Second, it could help people be healthier and live longer. If doctors had access to their patients' DNA information, they might be able to determine what diseases a patient might get. For example, DNA information might tell a doctor that a patient is likely to develop cancer. Then that patient could receive cancer screenings every year in order to catch the cancer and treat it in its early stages.

b Some people believe strongly in the importance of national DNA databanks. Others don't believe that DNA databanks should exist. People on both sides of the issue have strong reasons for their opinions. In fact, the topic has sparked many debates in the legal community. If people were required to give DNA samples that were to be kept in a national databank, it would save time and money. Currently in many countries, people cannot be forced to provide a DNA sample, even if they are accused of a crime. With a DNA databank, police might be able to identify criminals more quickly and easily if they had access to everyone's DNA information. Investigations could take less time and fewer resources, and this would save the government and taxpayers money. Second, it could help people be healthier and live longer.

D | Critical Thinking: Analyzing. Work with a partner. Compare the two paragraphs by answering the following questions about each one. Check (✓) the column(s).

		a		b	
1.	Does the paragraph have one main idea?	Y	N	Y	N
2.	Is there a topic sentence that states the writer's opinion about the topic?	Y	N	Y	N
3.	Does the paragraph include at least two reasons for the writer's opinion?	Y	N	Y	N
4.	Are there details and examples that support both reasons?	Y	N	Y	N
5.	Are modals of obligation and possibility used correctly?	Y	N	Y	N

Now discuss your answer to this question: Which paragraph is better? Why?

E | Revising. Answer the questions above about your own paragraph.

F | Peer Evaluation. Exchange your first draft with a partner and follow the steps below.

Step 1 Read your partner's paragraph and tell him or her one thing that you liked about it.

Step 2 Complete the idea map below showing your partner's opinion, supporting ideas, and details.

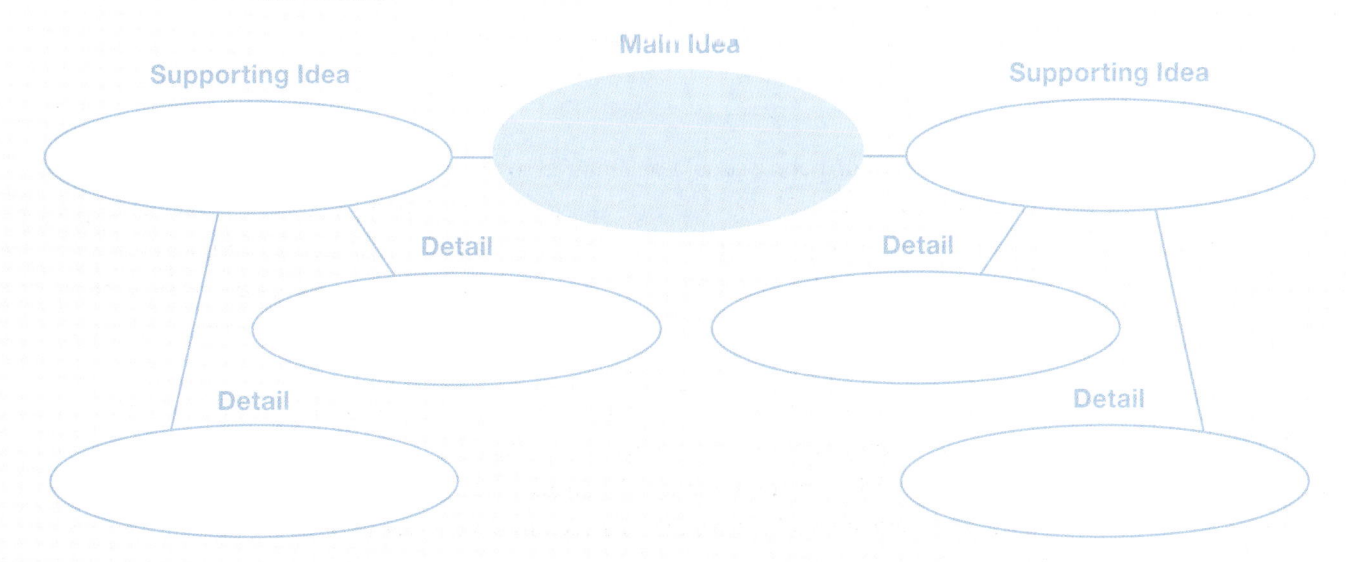

LESSON C
WRITING TASK: Editing

Step 3 Compare this idea map with the one that your partner created in exercise **A** on page 44.

Step 4 The two idea maps should be similar. If they aren't, discuss how they differ.

G | Draft 2. Write a second draft of your paragraph. Use what you learned from the peer evaluation activity and your answers to exercise **E**. Make any other necessary changes.

H | Editing Practice. Read the information in the box. Then find and correct one mistake with modals of obligation and possibility in each of the sentences (1–5).

> With modals of obligation and possibility, remember to:
> - use *should* or *should not* to express an opinion about the best thing to do or not to do (obligation).
> - use *might* or *could* to show potential (possible) results of an action.
> - follow a modal with the base form of a verb.

1. If governments had national DNA databanks, police could finding criminals more easily.
2. In my opinion, no one could have to give DNA samples to the police.
3. Dishonest detectives might going to use DNA information in illegal ways.
4. I think researchers could continue to study the Iceman to learn more about the lives of people in prehistoric times.
5. Some researchers want to do CT scans of other pharaohs' mummies. It is possible the scans should prove how the pharaohs died.

I | Editing Checklist. Use the checklist to find errors in your second draft.

Editing Checklist   Yes   No

1. Are all the words spelled correctly?
2. Is the first word of every sentence capitalized?
3. Does every sentence end with the correct punctuation?
4. Do your subjects and verbs agree?
5. Did you use modals of obligation and possibility correctly?
6. Are verb tenses correct?

J | Final Draft. Now use your Editing Checklist to write a third draft of your paragraph. Make any other necessary changes.

UNIT 3

City Solutions

ACADEMIC PATHWAYS
Lesson A: Identifying reasons
Evaluating sources
Lesson B: Reading an interview
Lesson C: Writing a thesis statement
Writing descriptive paragraphs

Think and Discuss

1. What are the biggest cities in your country? Describe them.
2. What is your favorite city? What do you like about it?

▲ An aerial view of Kowloon, Hong Kong

Exploring the Theme

A. Look at the maps and discuss the questions.

1. What was the largest city in 1900? In 1950? In 2010?
2. How many people live in the largest city today?
3. In which time period did cities grow the fastest—from 1900 to 1950, or from 1950 to 2010? What are some possible causes of urban growth?

B. Read the information and discuss the questions.

1. Where are the fastest-growing cities today?
2. What are two things that contribute to the growth of cities today?

People crowd the Churchgate Railway Station in Mumbai, the world's densest city.

Rise of the Cities

Urban centers of more than a million people were rare until the early 20th century. Today there are 21 cities of more than ten million people. Almost all of these large cities—called megacities—are in the developing regions of Asia, Africa, and Latin America. Cities in these regions are likely to grow even bigger in the future as populations rise and migration from rural areas continues. Some urban areas in West Africa, China, and India contain several overlapping cities, forming huge urban networks with more than 50 million people.

Dots represent cities with a population of more than one million people. Populations of the largest cities are indicated in millions.

1900 — 16 cities
- Chicago, U.S. 1.7
- 4.2 New York, U.S.
- 6.5 London, U.K.
- 2.7 Berlin, Germany
- 3.3 Paris, France

1950 — 74 cities
- 12.3 New York
- Paris 6.5
- 8.4 London
- 5.4 Moscow, U.S.S.R.
- 11.3 Tokyo, Japan

2010 — 442 cities
- 20.3 Mexico City, Mexico
- 20.3 São Paulo, Brazil
- 22.2 Delhi, India
- 20.0 Mumbai, India
- 36.7 Tokyo, Japan

CITY SOLUTIONS

LESSON A   PREPARING TO READ

A | Building Vocabulary. Find the words in **blue** in the reading passage on pages 51–53. Use the context to guess their meanings. Then match the sentence parts below to make definitions.

1. _d_ An **aspect** of something is
2. _f_ A **decade** is
3. _j_ If a person or thing **enables** you to do something,
4. _g_ To **exceed** a particular amount
5. _i_ If you **focus** on a particular topic,
6. _h_ A person's **income** is
7. _b_ If something is **inevitable**,
8. _e_ The **infrastructure** of a country is
9. _a_ An **institute** is
10. _c_ If a government **invests** money in an organization,

a. an organization or building where a particular type of work is done, especially research and teaching.
b. it is certain to happen and cannot be prevented or avoided.
c. it provides money to help it grow.
d. one of the parts of its character or nature.
e. its basic facilities, such as transportation, communications, power supplies, and buildings.
f. a period of ten years.
g. is to be greater than that amount.
h. the money that he or she earns or receives.
i. you concentrate on it and deal with it.
j. it makes it possible for you to do it.

Word Partners

Use **income**
with: (*adj.*) **average** income, **large/small** income, **steady** income, **taxable** income; (*v.*) **earn** an income, **supplement** your income; (*n.*) **loss** of income, **source** of income

---

B | Using Vocabulary. Answer the questions. Share your ideas with a partner.

1. What are your plans for the next **decade**? Will you live in the same area? What kind of work do you plan to do? How do you plan to earn an **income**?
2. Which problems in your city do you think people should **focus** on right now?
3. What changes in technology do you think are **inevitable** over the next decade?

C | Brainstorming. Discuss your answers to these questions, in small groups.

What are some advantages to living in cities? What are some disadvantages?

D | Predicting. Skim the reading passage on pages 51–53. Read the title, the headings, and the first and last sentences of each paragraph. What is the reading passage mainly about? Complete the sentence below. As you read, check your prediction.

I think the reading is about the **positive/negative** aspects of living in cities and ways to manage _____ in cities in the future.

50 | UNIT 3

READING

Living on an Urban Planet

▲ People crowd a narrow street lined with shops in Harajuku, Tokyo.

CONSIDER THIS: In 1800, less than three percent of the world's population lived in cities. Only one city—Beijing, China—had a population of more than a million people. Most people lived in rural areas, and many spent their entire lives without ever seeing a city. In 1900, just a hundred years later, roughly 150 million people lived in cities. By then, the world's ten largest urban areas all had populations exceeding one million; London—the world's largest—had more than six million people. By 2000, the number of people living in cities had exceeded three billion; and, in 2008, the world's population crossed a tipping point[1] more than one-half of the people on Earth lived in cities. By 2050, that could increase to more than two-thirds. The trend is clear and the conclusion inescapable—humans have become an urban species.

[1] A **tipping point** is a point in time when a very important change occurs.
[2] **Breeding grounds** are places that encourage the growth and development of certain conditions.

Cities as Solutions

In the 19th and early 20th centuries, as large urban areas began to grow and spread, many people viewed cities largely in negative terms—as crowded, dirty, unhealthy environments that were breeding grounds[2] for disease and crime. People feared that as cities got bigger, living conditions would get worse. Recent decades, however, have seen a widespread change in attitude toward urbanization. To a growing number of economists, urban planners, and environmentalists, urbanization is good news. Though negative aspects such as pollution and urban slums remain serious problems, many planners now believe big cities offer a solution to dealing with the problem of Earth's growing population.

Harvard economist Edward Glaeser is one person who believes that cities bring largely positive benefits. Glaeser's optimism is reflected in the title of his book *The Triumph of the City*. Glaeser argues that poor

LESSON A   READING

people flock to cities because that's usually where the money is. Cities are productive because of "the absence of space between people," which reduces the cost of transporting goods, people, and ideas. While the flow of goods has always been important to cities, what is most important today is the flow of ideas. Successful cities attract and reward smart people with higher wages, and they enable people to learn from one another. According to Glaeser, a perfect example of how information can be exchanged in an urban environment is the trading floor of the New York Stock Exchange on Wall Street (pictured above). There, employees work in one open, crowded space sharing information. "They value knowledge over space. That's what the modern city is all about."

Another champion[3] of urbanization is environmentalist Stewart Brand. From an ecological perspective,[4] says Brand, moving people out of cities would be disastrous. Because cities are dense, they allow half of the world's population to live on about four percent of the land, leaving more space for open country, such as farmland. People living in cities also have less impact per capita[5] on the environment. Their roads, sewers,[6] and power lines are shorter and require fewer resources to build and operate. City apartments require less energy to heat, cool, and light than larger houses in suburbs and rural areas. Most importantly, people living in dense cities drive less. They can walk to many destinations, and public transportation is practical because enough people travel regularly to the same places. As a result, dense cities tend to produce fewer greenhouse gas emissions per person than scattered, sprawling[7] suburbs.

Because of these reasons, it is a mistake to see urbanization as evil; instead, we should view it as an inevitable part of development, says David Satterwaite of London's International Institute of Environment and Development. For Satterwaite and other urban planners, rapid growth itself is not the real problem—the larger issue is how to manage the growth. There is no one model for how to manage rapid urbanization, but there are hopeful examples. One is Seoul, South Korea.

Seoul's Success Story

Between 1960 and 2000, Seoul's population increased from fewer than three million to ten million people. In the same period, South Korea went from being one of the world's poorest countries, with a per capita GDP (Gross Domestic Product) of less than $100, to being richer than some countries in Europe. How could this rapid urbanization produce such

GREENHOUSE GAS EMISSIONS PER PERSON
Tons of CO_2 equivalent; Sample years 1994–2007

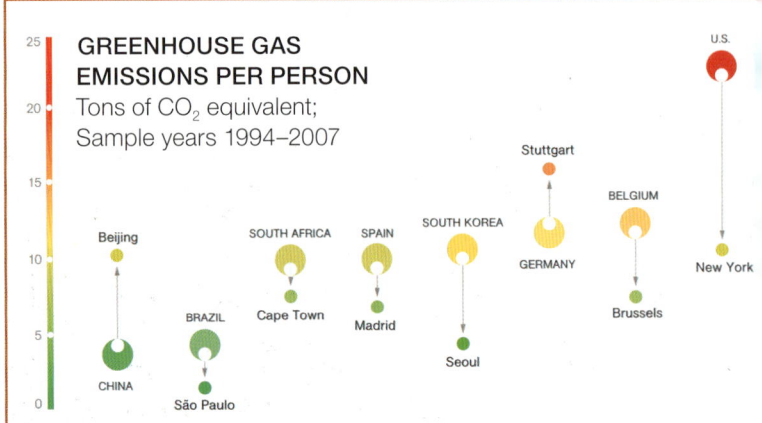

▲ **City-Country Gap:** In most cases, large, dense cities tend to emit less CO_2 per person than their national average.

52 | UNIT 3

economic growth? Large numbers of people first began arriving in Seoul in the 1950s. The government soon recognized that economic development was essential for supporting its growing urban population. It began to invest capital[8] in South Korean companies that made products that foreigners wanted to buy—at first, inexpensive clothing and later, steel, electronics, and cars. This investment eventually helped large, modern corporations such as Samsung and Hyundai to grow and develop. Central to South Korea's economic success were the men and women pouring into Seoul to work in its new factories. "You can't understand urbanization in isolation from economic development," says economist Kyung-Hwan Kim of Sogang University. The expanding city enabled economic growth, which paid for the buildings, roads, and other infrastructure that helped the city absorb even more people.

Seoul today is one of the densest cities in the world. It has millions of cars, but it also has an excellent subway system. Overall, life has gotten much better for South Koreans during the past few decades of rapid urbanization. Life expectancy has increased from 51 years in 1961 to 79 years today. South Korea's transformation into a country with great economic power cannot be easily copied, but it proves that a poor country can urbanize successfully and incredibly fast.

Managing Urbanization

Despite success stories such as Seoul, urban planners around the world continue to struggle with the problem of how to manage urbanization. While they used to worry mainly about city density—the large number of people living closely together—urban planners today are increasingly focusing on urban sprawl—the way big cities are spreading out and taking over more and more land.

Shlomo Angel, an urban planning professor at New York University and Princeton University, sees two main reasons for urban sprawl—rising incomes and cheaper transportation. "When income rises, people have money to buy more space," he says. With cheaper transportation, people can afford to travel longer distances to work. In the second half of the 20th century, for example, many people in the United States moved from apartments in cities to houses in suburban areas, where they depend more on cars for transportation. This trend has led to expanding suburbs, which has led to greater energy use as well as increased air pollution and greenhouse gas emissions.

Today, many planners want to bring people back to cities and make suburbs denser by creating walkable town centers, high-rise apartment buildings, and more public transportation so people are less dependent on cars. "It would be a lot better for the planet," says Edward Glaeser, if people are "in dense cities built around the elevator rather than in sprawling areas built around the car."

Shlomo Angel believes that planning can make a big difference in the way cities are allowed to grow. However, good planning requires looking decades ahead, says Angel, and reserving land—before the city grows over it—for parks and public transportation space. It also requires, as in the example of Seoul, looking at growing cities in a positive way—as concentrations of human energy. With the Earth's population headed toward nine or ten billion, dense and carefully planned cities are looking more like a solution—perhaps the best hope for lifting people out of poverty without wrecking[9] the planet.

▲ In 1961, just 28 percent of Koreans lived in cities; today, Korea's population is more than 80 percent urban.

[3] If you are a **champion** of something, you support or defend it.
[4] A **perspective** is a way of thinking about something.
[5] **Per capita** means per person—for example, the impact per person that people living in cities have on the environment.
[6] **Sewers** are large underground channels that carry waste matter and rainwater away.
[7] If something is **sprawling**, it is growing outward in an uncontrolled way.
[8] **Capital** is cash or goods used to generate income, usually by investing in business or in property.
[9] To **wreck** something means to completely destroy or ruin it.

LESSON A — UNDERSTANDING THE READING

A | Identifying Main Ideas. Skim the reading again. Choose the sentence in each pair that *best expresses* the main idea.

1. Paragraph A:
   a. Less than three percent of the world's population lived in cities in 1800.
   ✓ b. More than one-half of the people on Earth now live in cities.

2. Paragraph B:
   ✓ a. In recent decades, attitudes toward living in cities have changed.
   b. In the 19th century, many people viewed cities negatively.

3. Paragraph C:
   a. Successful cities attract and reward smart people.
   ✓ b. Cities bring largely positive benefits.

4. Paragraph D:
   ✓ a. Urbanization is good for the environment.
   b. People living in dense cities drive less.

5. Paragraph E:
   a. Seoul, South Korea, is an example of how to manage rapid urbanization.
   ✓ b. The biggest issue facing urban planners is how to manage urban growth. [= problem]

6. Paragraph G:
   a. Seoul has millions of cars, but it also has an excellent transportation system.
   ✓ b. Overall, life has improved for Koreans during the decades of rapid urbanization.

7. Paragraph K:
   a. Planning requires looking at cities in a positive way.
   ✓ b. Planning can make a big difference in the way cities are allowed to grow.

B | Identifying Key Details. Answer the questions about details in "Living on an Urban Planet."

1. What fraction of the world's population could live in cities by 2050? (Paragraph A)

   More than two-third w. pop

2. Why did many people view cities in negative terms in the 19th and early 20th centuries? (Paragraph B)

   b/c they feared that city bigger → living cond. worse; pollution, urban slum

3. According to Edward Glaeser, what are two benefits of living in cities? (Paragraph C)

   1. Reduce cost of transporting goods, people, idea
   2. Earn higher wages

4. According to Stewart Brand, what is one benefit of dense cities? (Paragraph D)

   People live in dense cities have less impact per capita on the environment

5. How did economic growth help Seoul make room for the increasing number of people who came to the city? (Paragraph F)

   - paid for building roads, infrastructure
   - invest money into companies

54 | UNIT 3

6. What is "urban sprawl"? (Paragraph H)

   uncontrolled development of city

7. According to Shlomo Angel, what are two causes of urban sprawl? (Paragraph I)

   rising income & cheaper transportation

8. What are two ways to make people less dependent on cars in cities? (Paragraph J)

   1. Create walkable town centers, mixed use apartment buildings
   2. more public transportation

> **CT Focus:** Evaluating Sources
>
> Writers often **quote or paraphrase** the ideas of experts to support information in an article. When writers quote an idea, they write the expert's exact words in quotation marks. When writers paraphrase, they write the expert's idea in their own words and do not use quotation marks. Writers often introduce a quote or paraphrase with *According to . . .* or *[he/she] thinks/says/believes . . . .* When you read a quote or paraphrase from an expert, ask yourself these questions: What are the expert's credentials—that is, his or her profession or area of expertise? How do the quotes or paraphrases support the writer's main ideas? How do they strengthen the writer's arguments?

C | Critical Thinking: Evaluating Sources. Find the following four quotes and paraphrases in "Living on an Urban Planet." Note the paragraph where you find each one. Then discuss with a partner your answers to the questions below.

1. _____ According to Glaeser, a perfect example of how information can be exchanged in an urban environment is the trading floor of the New York Stock Exchange on Wall Street. "They value knowledge over space. That's what the modern city is all about."

2. _____ From an ecological perspective, says Brand, moving people out of cities would be disastrous.

3. _____ Shlomo Angel . . . sees two main reasons for urban sprawl—rising incomes and cheaper transportation. "When income rises, people have money to buy more space," he says.

4. _____ Shlomo Angel believes that planning can make a big difference in the way cities are allowed to grow. However, good planning requires looking decades ahead, says Angel, and reserving land—before the city grows over it—for parks and public transportation space.

1. Circle the direct quotes. Underline the paraphrases.
2. What idea does each quote or paraphrase support?
3. Does the writer give the experts' credentials? What are their credentials?
4. How does the quote/paraphrase strengthen the writer's arguments?

D | Personalizing. Write an answer to the following question: Do you agree that city life is mainly beneficial? Why, or why not?

LESSON A   DEVELOPING READING SKILLS

Reading Skill: Identifying Reasons

Writers give reasons to explain and support their main ideas. When you look for reasons that support and explain ideas, look for information that answers the questions "Why?," "How?," or "What is one reason that . . . ?" Look at this example from Paragraph C on pages 51–52:

Main idea: Cities are mostly beneficial. **Question**: Why?

The writer supports this idea with many reasons, including the following: *Successful cities attract and reward smart people with higher wages, and they enable people to learn from one another.*

A | Understanding Reasons. Read the two paragraphs. Answer the questions that follow. Then underline the information in the paragraphs that gives you the answers.

People who live in areas affected by urban sprawl tend to rely more on cars to get to school and work or to go shopping. Urban sprawl also increases road traffic as people increasingly rely on roads and highways. As a result, suburban residents not only use more energy, they face longer commutes and are more dependent on fossil fuels, such as gas, than people who live in cities.

- What is one reason that people who live in suburbs use more energy than people who live in cities?

  _____

"Smart growth" is an approach to development aimed at addressing the problems caused by urban sprawl. In smart-growth communities, new development involves creating downtown areas that combine housing with commercial areas and places of entertainment. Because the places where they work, shop, and relax are close together, residents can use low-energy forms of transportation, such as walking, biking, and public transportation, to get around. Creating these kinds of energy-efficient communities helps residents save time and money, and reduces the demand for natural resources such as fossil fuels.

- How can smart growth help people use fewer resources?

  _____

B | Applying. Reread Paragraph D on page 52. Find and underline reasons that support the main idea: *Urbanization is good for the environment.* Then answer the questions.

1. Why would it be a bad idea for people to move out of cities?

   _____

   _____

2. How do people who live in cities save energy?

   _____

   _____

3. Why do dense cities produce fewer greenhouse gas emissions than suburbs do?

   _____

   _____

VIEWING

Solar Solutions

▲ Houses and rooftops of Cairo, Egypt

Before Viewing

A | Using a Dictionary. Here are some words and expressions you will hear in the video. Match each word or expression with the correct definition. Use your dictionary to help you.

> 3 a no-brainer   1 cut down on   5 dwellers   4 found materials   2 going green

1. _____: reduce or decrease
2. _____: living in an environmentally responsible way
3. _____: something that is easy to understand
4. _____: objects in the environment that people can use for various purposes
5. _____: people who live in a place

B | Thinking Ahead. Discuss these questions with a partner: Where in a house or an apartment building might be a good location for a solar-powered water heater? What might be the advantages of using solar-powered water heaters?

While Viewing

Read questions 1–5. Think about the answers as you view the video.

1. What does Culhane use to make solar-powered water heaters?
2. Why do solar-powered water heaters work so well in Cairo?
3. What advantages do solar-powered water heaters give to the people using them?
4. What is one problem with using solar-powered heaters in Cairo? Why is it a problem?
5. At the end of the video, the narrator says: "One man's garbage is another man's treasure." What do you think this means?

After Viewing

A | Discuss your answers to questions 1–5 above with a partner.

B | Critical Thinking: Synthesizing. Think about the reading passage "Living on an Urban Planet." Explain how the rooftops of Cairo are an example of a "city solution." What problems do Cairo rooftops help to solve?

LESSON B PREPARING TO READ

A | Building Vocabulary. Find the words in blue in the reading passage on pages 59–61. Use the context to guess their meanings. Then write each word below next to its definition (1–10).

> consistent   consumption   enhance   fundamental   justified
> majority   objective   phenomenon statistical   sustain

1. _____: (verb) continue or maintain something for a period of time
2. _____: (noun) something that is observed to happen or exist
3. _____: (adjective) reasonable or acceptable, for example, a decision or an action
4. _____: (noun) more than half of people or things in a group
5. _____: (noun) the act of using something, for example, energy or food
6. _____: (adjective) based on facts, not feelings or opinions
7. _____: (verb) improve
8. _____: (adjective) expressed in numbers
9. _____: (adjective) always behaving or appearing in the same way
10. _____: (adjective) things or ideas that are very important or essential

B | Using Vocabulary. Discuss these questions with a partner.

1. What subjects do the **majority** of students in your school study?
2. How do parks **enhance** the quality of life in cities?
3. Are people in your city concerned about energy **consumption**? Why, or why not?
4. Is telling a lie ever **justified**? If yes, in what situations?
5. In your opinion, is free speech a **fundamental** human right? Explain your answer.

C | Predicting. Skim the reading passage on pages 59–61. Read the first paragraph and the interview questions. Which topics do you think the interview covers? As you read, check your predictions.

1. _____ a study on urbanization
2. _____ why people live in cities
3. _____ facts about some of the cities in the study
4. _____ the history of the modern city
5. _____ urban architecture

Word Partners

Use **majority** with: (adj.) **overwhelming** majority, **vast** majority; (n.) majority **of people**, majority **of the population**

READING

THE URBAN VISIONARY

For the first time in history, the world's population is mostly urban. Richard Wurman decided to find out what that really means.

WHEN ARCHITECT AND URBAN PLANNER Richard Wurman learned that the majority of Earth's population lived in cities, he became curious. He wondered what the effects will be of global urbanization. With a group of business and media partners, Wurman set out on a five-year study—a project called 19.20.21—to collect information about urbanization, focusing on the world's largest urban concentrations, or megacities.

The project's aim is to standardize the way information about cities—such as health, education, transportation, energy consumption, and arts and culture—is collected and shared. The hope is that urban planners will be able to use these objective data to enhance the quality of life for people in cities while reducing the environmental impact of urbanization.

Q. What draws people to cities?

Wurman: People flock to cities because of the possibilities for doing things that interest them. Those interests—and the economics that make them possible—are based on people living together. We really have turned into a world of cities. Cities cooperate with each other. Cities trade with each other. Cities are where you put museums, where you put universities, where you put the centers of government, the centers of corporations. The inventions, the discoveries, the music and art in our world all take place in these intense gatherings of individuals.

Q. Tell us about 19.20.21.

Wurman: For the first time in history, more people . . . live in cities than outside them. I thought I'd try to discover what this new phenomenon really means. I went to the Web, and I tried to find the appropriate books and lists that would give me information, data, maps, so I could understand. And I couldn't find what I was looking for. I couldn't find maps of cities to the same scale. Much of the statistical information is gathered independently by each city, and the questions they ask are often not the same . . . There's no readily available information on the speed of growth of cities. Diagrams on power, water distribution and quality, health care, and education aren't available, so a metropolis[1] can't find out any information about itself relative to other cities and, therefore, can't judge the success or failure of programs . . .

[1] A **metropolis** is a large, important, busy city.

CITY SOLUTIONS | 59

LESSON B READING

E So I decided to gather consistent information on 19 cities that will have more than 20 million people in the 21st century. That's what 19.20.21 is about. We'll have a varied group of young cities, old cities, third-world cities, second-world cities, first-world cities, fast-growing cities, slow-growing cities, coastal cities, inland cities, industrial cities, [and] cultural cities . . . so that cities around the world can see themselves relative to others.

Q. What are some of the cities you're looking at?

F **Wurman:** What inspires me is being able to understand something, and understanding often comes from looking at extremes. So the cities that pop out are the ones that are clearly the largest, the oldest, the fastest growing, the lowest, the highest, the densest, the least dense, [or] the largest in area. The densest city is Mumbai. The fastest growing is Lagos. For years, the largest city was Mexico City, but Tokyo is now the biggest . . . There are cities that are basically spread out, like Los Angeles. Then there are classic cities, which you certainly wouldn't want to leave out, like Paris. I find the data on cities to be endlessly fascinating. Just look at the world's ten largest cities through time. The biggest city in the year 1000 was Córdoba, Spain. Beijing was the biggest city in 1500 and 1800, London in 1900, New York City in 1950, and today [it's] Tokyo.

Q. Cities are increasingly challenged to sustain their infrastructure and service. Can they survive as they are now?

G **Wurman:** Nothing survives as it is now. All cities are cities for the moment, and our thoughts about how to make them better are thoughts at the moment. There was great passion 30 years ago for the urban bulldozer,[2] that we had to tear down the slums, tear down the old parts of cities, and have urban renewal. That lasted for about 10, 15 years, until it didn't seem to work very well. And yet the reasons for doing it seemed justified at that moment . . . It shows that the attempt to make things better often makes things worse. We have to understand before we act. And although there are a lot of little ideas for making things better—better learning, increased safety, cleaner air—you can't solve the problem with a collection of little ideas. One has to understand them in context and in comparison to other places.

▲ Street market in Lagos, Nigeria, the world's fastest-growing city

[2] A **bulldozer** is a large vehicle used for knocking down buildings.

Guggenheim Museum, Bilbao, Spain

Q. **You're an architect by training. Do you agree with the U.K.'s Prince Charles that architects have ruined the urban landscape?[3]**

Wurman: You can point to examples where architecture has ruined the urban landscape, and you can point to places where architecture has been the fundamental positive change. Look at the [High Line] park that runs [along the Hudson River] on the west side of Manhattan. That was done by architects and urban planners. Has it ruined New York? No. It's the beginning of knitting parts of the place together and the recognition that you're on the water, and it's a healthy thing.

But there is too much bling[4] architecture—that's the showbiz[5] part of architecture. Even though these individual buildings might be wonderful, they are not necessarily wonderful within the fabric of the city.[6] Sometimes you can excuse them because they draw people from around the world to see them and, therefore, improve the health of the city. The classic example is Bilbao. Frank Gehry's [Guggenheim] museum in Bilbao draws millions of people and has changed this industrial Spanish city into a [center] for tourism. It's inspired other architects to improve the subway system and other buildings, and some of the wineries, and some of the hotels in and around the city. So that bling is certainly excusable.

But buildings that have nothing to do with the fabric of the city, that are brought about by the client's desire to have a signature building,[7] those are not, in the long run, healthy because the fabric is what makes the city. Venice's Piazza San Marco was made by the fabric of all the buildings around that incredible square with just one cathedral at the end.

[3] The **urban landscape** is the general appearance of a city.
[4] If something is **bling**, it is done in an exaggerated way, intended to impress people.
[5] **Showbiz** comes from "show business," or the entertainment industry. If something is **showbiz**, it is intended to impress people or get their attention
[6] **The fabric of a city** is its basic structure.
[7] A **signature building** is a building that symbolizes or defines a place, usually because it is very distinctive.

Piazza San Marco, Venice, Italy

CITY SOLUTIONS | 61

LESSON B
UNDERSTANDING THE READING

A | Identifying Main Ideas. Choose the sentence in each pair that best expresses some of the main ideas in Wurman's interview.

1. Paragraph C:
   - ✓ a. People come to cities because cities are where important activities are happening.
   - b. People come to cities because universities and government centers are there.

2. Paragraphs D and E:
   - a. I started the project because it's difficult to compare cities using maps.
   - ✓ b. I started the project because there's a need for consistent information about cities.

3. Paragraph F:
   - ✓ a. Studying the most extreme cities can help us get a better understanding of urbanization.
   - b. The world's largest city has changed several times during the last thousand years.

4. Paragraph I:
   - ✓ a. Some new architecture can improve the basic structure of a city.
   - b. Frank Gehry's Guggenheim Museum improved tourism in Bilbao.

B | Identifying Meaning from Context. Find and underline the following words and phrases in the reading passage on pages 59–61. Use context to help you identify the meaning of each word. Complete the definitions. Check your answers in a dictionary.

1. Paragraph C: When people **flock to** a place, they _gather_ in large numbers. *come together*

2. Paragraphs D and E: **Relative to** something means in _comparasion_ with it.

3. Paragraph F: If things **pop out**, they are very _obvious_ because they are unusual. ✓ *attract your eyes = stand out = clear*

4. Paragraph G: **Slums** are parts of cities where living conditions are very _poor_. *danken*

5. Paragraph H: **Knitting** things together is _joining_ /connecting them.
   = attract

6. Paragraph I: Things that **draw** people to a city make them want to _go there_.

7. Paragraph I: If something is **excusable**, you can understand and _____ it.

C | Identifying Supporting Details. Find details in the reading passage to answer the following questions.

The 19.20.21 Project (Paragraphs D–F)

1. What do the numbers in the title of Wurman's project mean (*19, 20,* and *21*)?
   19 cities that will have more than 20 million people in the 21st cent

2. What are some examples of cities that "pop out" to Wurman? Why do they "pop out"?
   Mumbai - densest city; fastest growing - Lagos, biggest - Tokyo

D | Identifying Reasons. Note answers to these questions. Then discuss your ideas with a partner.

1. Why was creating the High Line Park in New York City a positive change? (Paragraph H)
   B/c it's the beginning of knitting parts of the place together & recognition
   connect

2. Why does Wurman think there is too much "bling" architecture? (Paragraph I)
   B/c they not necessarily wonderful within the fabric of the city.

3. Why can you sometimes excuse "bling" architecture, according to Wurman? (Paragraph I)
   they draw p/p from around the world to see them &, therefore, improve the health of the city.

E | Critical Thinking: Evaluating Sources. Imagine that you are going to make recommendations for improving a city. Check (✓) the experts you would consult and give reasons for your choices. For each type of expert you check, answer the questions below. Share your ideas in a small group.

☐ architects   ☐ landscapers   ☐ entertainers
☐ urban planners   ☐ environmentalists   ☐ artists
☐ engineers   ☐ scientists   ☐ other: _____

1. What information would you want to get from the person?
2. What questions would you ask the person?

F | Critical Thinking: Synthesizing. Think about the passages you read in this unit and answer this question. Share your answer in a small group.

Which person do you think has the most positive view of cities—Edward Glaeser, Stewart Brand, Shlomo Angel, or Richard Wurman? Why? Give examples to support your opinion.

_____
_____
_____

G | Personalizing. Discuss your answers to these questions in small groups.

1. What are some famous signature buildings in cities around the world? How do they symbolize the places they are in?

2. What are some examples of expensive, unusual, or "bling" architecture in your city or in a city you are familiar with? Do you like these structures? Why, or why not?

LESSON C — EXPLORING WRITTEN ENGLISH

GOAL: Writing Descriptive Paragraphs
In this lesson, you are going to plan, write, revise, and edit descriptive paragraphs on the following topic: *Describe two things that improved the quality of life in your city or a city you know.*

A | **Brainstorming.** Think of a city you know well that is better to live in now than it used to be. What was it like in the past? What is it like now? Think about architecture, environmental issues, public transportation, job opportunities, etc. Complete the chart with your ideas.

City _____

In the Past	Today

Free Writing. Write about what the city in your brainstorming notes is like today. Think about the things that make it a nice place to live. Write for five minutes.

B | Read the information in the box. Then use the cues to complete the sentences (1–4) with the correct simple past form of the verb, or *used to* + verb.

Language for Writing: Using the Simple Past and *used to*

When you describe a situation in the past, you usually use the simple past forms of verbs.

*Ten years ago, it **was** difficult to get around the city. People **drove** everywhere because there **was** no convenient public transportation. People **didn't walk** downtown because it was dangerous.*

We can also use *used to* to describe regular conditions and behavior in the past.

*People **used to drive** downtown instead of taking public transportation.*
*It **used to be** dangerous to walk in certain neighborhoods at night.*
*It **used to take** hours to get from one side of the city to the other.*

Use *used to* with the base form of the verb.

See page 247 for a list of irregular past verb forms.

1. There / be / a lot of air pollution. (*used to*)

   _____

2. The buses / run / on gasoline. (simple past)

   _____

3. We / not have / a sports team in my city. (simple past)

   _____

4. Downtown / look / very unattractive. (*used to*)

   _____

C | Applying. Write about past conditions in the city you thought about in your brainstorming notes. Write three affirmative sentences and two negative sentences. Use the simple past and *used to*.

> **Writing Skill:** Writing a Thesis Statement
>
> A paragraph typically expresses one main idea. When you write an essay, you will present several main ideas. Each main idea appears in **body paragraphs**, the main part of an essay. An essay also includes an introductory paragraph. This paragraph gives general information about the topic, and it includes a **thesis statement**, which is a statement that expresses the idea of the entire essay. A good thesis statement has the following characteristics:
>
> - It presents your position or opinion on the topic.
> - It includes the reasons for your opinion or position on the topic.
> - It expresses only the ideas that you can easily explain in your body paragraphs.
> - It includes key words that connect with the topic sentences of the body paragraphs.
>
> *The quality of life in Morristown is better today than it was in the past* because we now
>   **Opinion**
> have *a more convenient bus system* and *pedestrian-only streets downtown*.
>   **Reason 1**   **Reason 2**
>
> Topic sentence for first body paragraph:
>   *A more convenient bus system is one thing that has improved life in Morristown.*
>
> Topic sentence for second body paragraph:
>   *Having pedestrian-only streets in the downtown area is another change that has made life better.*

D | Critical Thinking: Analyzing. Read the following pairs of thesis statements. Check the one in each pair that you think is better. Share your answers with a partner.

1. a. _____ Life is a lot better in Philadelphia than it was a few years ago for several good reasons.
   b. _____ Life is a lot better in Philadelphia today because there is less crime and more job opportunities.

2. a. _____ Two recent changes have improved the city of San Pedro—new streetlights and better roads.
   b. _____ Most residents of San Pedro are very pleased with the recent infrastructure improvements.

E | Applying. Decide what your opinion is on each topic below and give two reasons for each opinion. Use your opinions and your reasons to write two thesis statements.

1. Are primates and office workers similar in any way?
   My opinion: _____
   Reason 1: _____ Reason 2: _____
   Thesis statement: _____

2. Should people conduct scientific research on mummies?
   My opinion: _____
   Reason 1: _____ Reason 2: _____
   Thesis statement: _____

LESSON C
WRITING TASK: Drafting and Revising

A | Planning. Follow the steps to make notes for your paragraphs.

Step 1 Write the name of the city you are going to discuss in the chart below. Look at your brainstorming notes and choose the two most important things that make this city a better place to live today. Write these two things in the outline.

Step 2 Complete the thesis statement in the outline.

Step 3 Write topic sentences for each of your body paragraphs. In your topic sentences, use the key words in the reasons that you circled in your thesis statement.

Step 4 Now write two (or more) examples or details for the supporting ideas in each body paragraph.

City: _____

Two things that make it a better place to live: _____

_____

_____

Thesis statement: The quality of life in _____ is better today than it was in the past because _____ and _____.

Body Paragraph 1: Topic sentence: _____ is one thing that has improved life in _____.

Supporting Idea 1: _____

_____

Supporting Idea 2: _____

_____

Supporting Idea 3: _____

_____

Body Paragraph 2: Topic sentence: _____ has also improved life in _____.

Supporting Idea 1: _____

_____

Supporting Idea 2: _____

_____

Supporting Idea 3: _____

_____

Ideas for Introduction: _____

_____

Step 5 Think of some general information about your city: Where is it located? How many people live there? What do most people know about it? Write these ideas on the lines after "Ideas for Introduction."

B | Draft 1. Use the notes in your chart to write a first draft.

C | Critical Thinking: Analyzing. Work with a partner. Read the paragraphs about changes in San Francisco. Then follow the steps to analyze the paragraphs.

Introduction

San Francisco is a large city in Northern California. It has always been a nice place to live because it has beautiful architecture and good weather. However, two recent changes have made the city an even better place to live—<u>underground electrical wires</u> and <u>new bike lanes</u>.

Body Paragraph 1

topic
(Putting electrical wires underground) is one thing that has improved the appearance of San Francisco. In the past, the city used to have above-ground electrical wires hanging across every street.✗ The wires hung on tall wooden poles that were placed on every block.✗ The poles and the wires were unattractive.✗ For example, in one neighborhood, North Beach, they blocked people's view of the sky, the trees, and the beautiful Victorian apartment buildings that lined the streets.✓ Then, a few years ago, the city put all the electrical wires underground. This made the streets look much better. Today, people can enjoy the beautiful views as they walk down the streets in most San Francisco neighborhoods.

Body Paragraph 2

topic
(Creating new bike lanes) has also improved the quality of life in San Francisco. It ✗used to be dangerous to ride a bike in some areas of the city. Because they had to share the same lanes, cars and bikes were competing for space, and drivers injured many cyclists. ✓In 2010, the city created special biking lanes going into and out of the downtown areas. These lanes encouraged more people to ride bikes instead of driving their cars downtown. Bike riding reduces the number of cars, so there's less traffic downtown now. Fewer cars on the road mean fewer greenhouse gas emissions, so the air quality is better in the city, too.

Step 1 Underline the thesis statement in the introduction.

Step 2 Circle the two reasons in the thesis statement that support the writer's position or opinion on the topic.

Step 3 Underline the topic sentences in the two body paragraphs.

Step 4 Circle the key words in each topic sentence that match the key words in the thesis statement.

Step 5 In the first body paragraph, put an ✗ next to sentences that explain the way things used to be in the city. Check (✓) the sentences that describe changes.

Step 6 Repeat Step 5 for the second body paragraph.

D | Revising. Follow steps 1–6 in exercise **C** to analyze your own paragraphs.

E | Peer Evaluation. Exchange your first draft with a partner and follow the steps below.

Step 1 Read your partner's paragraphs and tell him or her one thing that you liked about them.

Step 2 Complete the chart on the next page based on your partner's paragraphs.

LESSON C

WRITING TASK: Editing

City: _____

Two things that make it a better place to live: _____

Thesis statement: The quality of life in _____ is better today than it was in the past because _____ and _____.

Body Paragraph 1: Topic sentence: _____ is one thing that has improved life in _____.

Supporting Ideas: _____

Body Paragraph 2: Topic sentence: _____ has also improved life in _____.

Supporting Ideas: _____

Step 3 Compare this outline with the one that your partner created in exercise **A** on page 66.

Step 4 The two outlines should be similar. If they aren't, discuss how they differ.

F | Draft 2. Write a second draft of your paragraphs. Use what you learned from the peer evaluation activity and your answers to exercise **D**. Make any other necessary changes.

G | Editing Practice. Read the information in the box. Then find and correct one mistake with the simple past or *used to* in each of the sentences (1–4).

> In sentences with the simple past and *used to*, remember to:
> - follow *used to* with the base form of the verb.
> - use the correct past forms for irregular verbs.

1. The Empire State Building used need a lot of energy, but now it is more energy-efficient.
2. The creek in downtown Seoul used to being covered in cement, but the city restored it.
3. Bangkok used to was very noisy, but the cars and motorcycles are much quieter now.
4. No buses runned in the downtown area, and this caused a lot of traffic.

H | Editing Checklist. Use the checklist to find errors in your second draft.

Editing Checklist Yes No

1. Are all the words spelled correctly?
2. Is the first word of every sentence capitalized?
3. Does every sentence end with the correct punctuation?
4. Do your subjects and verbs agree?
5. Did you use the simple past and *used to* correctly?
6. Are other verb tenses correct?

I | Final Draft. Now use your Editing Checklist to write a third draft of your paragraphs. Make any other necessary changes.

Danger Zones

UNIT 4

ACADEMIC PATHWAYS

Lesson A: Organizing your notes
Analyzing and evaluating evidence
Lesson B: Interpreting information in a multimodal text
Lesson C: Writing an introductory paragraph
Writing a set of paragraphs

Think and Discuss

1. What types of natural events can be dangerous to humans? Which are the most dangerous, and why?
2. Why do you think some people live in areas that are affected by extreme natural events?

▲ Children play on a swing within sight of the steaming volcano Popocatépetl in the state of Puebla, Mexico.

Exploring the Theme

A. Look at the map and the photos. What do you think the red areas show?

B. Read the information and check your answer to **A**. Then discuss the questions.

1. Where can you find the most earthquakes and volcanoes?
2. Where do most cyclones occur?
3. What do many of the places affected by natural hazards have in common?

World of Hazards

As this map shows, natural hazards tend to occur regularly in certain parts of the world. For example, most earthquakes and volcanoes occur at or near plate boundaries, whereas cyclones (large storm systems that cause coastal flooding) form in the tropics. Many of the world's most hazardous areas are also places with dense human populations.

(miles an hour)
186 or more
115-131

1 Earthquake

Port-au-Prince, Haiti

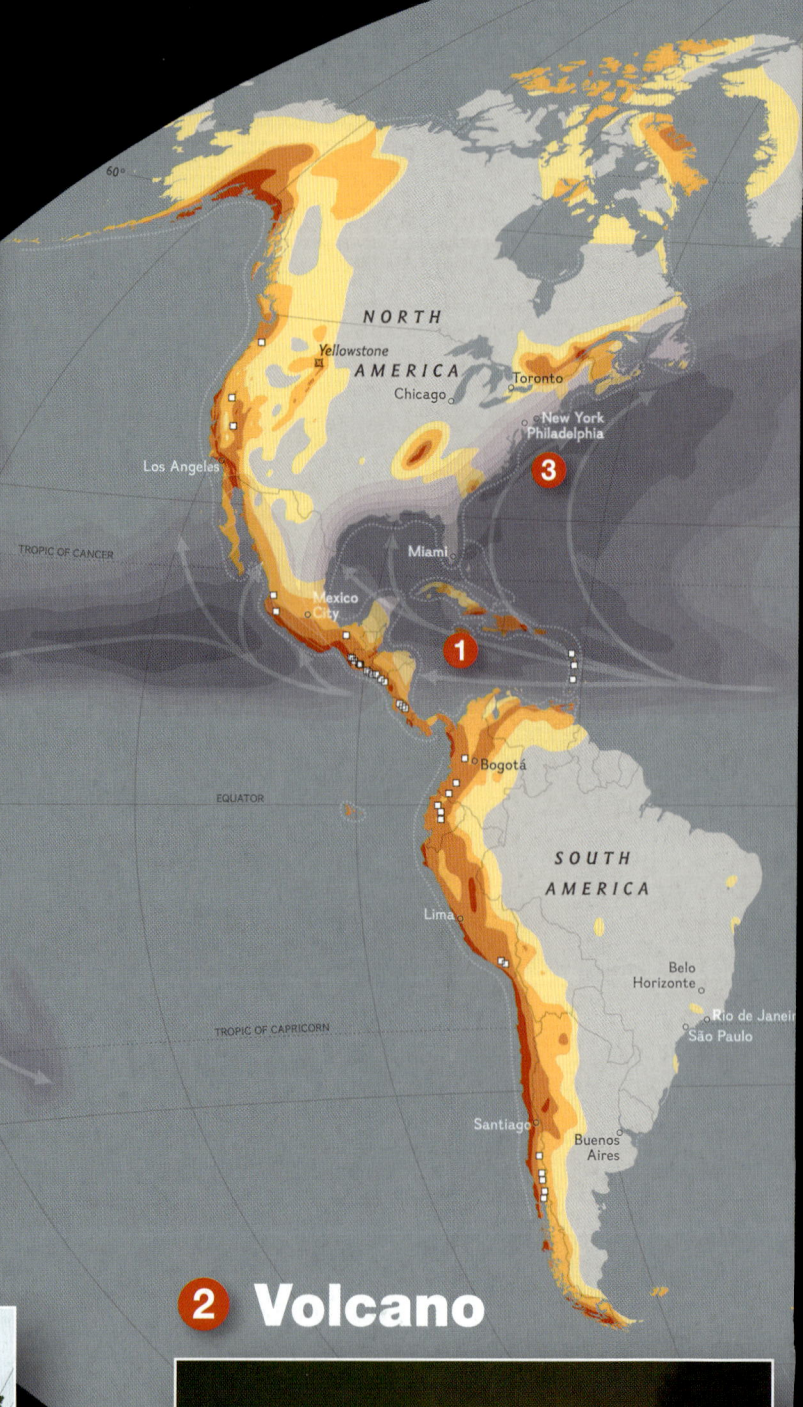

2 Volcano

4 Tsunami

Miyako, Iwate Prefecture, Japan

3 Cyclone

Hurricane Sandy heads toward the U.S.A.

Tropical cyclones
Wind speed
(miles an hour)

- 186 or more
- 157-185
- 132-156
- 115-131
- 88-114
- 47-87

← Typical path

Earthquake intensity
Modified Mercalli scale

- Catastrophic
- Destructive
- Very strong
- Strong
- Moderate

■ Most dangerous volcanoes

Tsunamis and storm surges
Coast vulnerable to inundation from a tsunami, storm surge, or both

Cities of five million or more shown

SAM PEPPLE, NGM STAFF
REWSEARCH: LISA R. RITTER, NGM STAFF; KAITLIN YARNALL, NGM STAFF
DATA: MÜNCHENER RÜCKVERSICHERUNGS-GESELLSCHAFT
Copyright © 2010

DANGER ZONES | 7

LESSON A | PREPARING TO READ

A | Building Vocabulary. Find the words in **blue** in the reading passage on pages 73–75. Use the context to guess their meanings. Then circle the correct word in each pair (1–10) to complete the paragraph.

Last year, there was an unusual **1.** commission / concentration of earthquakes in our area over a three-month period. This area is **2.** prone to / reluctant to earthquakes, but there hadn't been one in at least a decade. Many people were **3.** indicative / injured when some walls of older buildings fell. Our mayor recently set up a **4.** commission / concentration to investigate ways to raise money to repair the city's damaged historic buildings. When some citizens proposed tearing down some of the older buildings, the mayor's response was **5.** emphatic / reluctant: the buildings are important to the town's history, she argued, and must be protected. Her decision was supported by about half of the town's citizens. Only about a quarter of the town's population felt the buildings should be torn down and **6.** approximately / emphatically one-quarter didn't have an opinion. These days, most people think that the earthquakes have stopped at least for a while, but some locals are not **7.** convinced / reliable and are **8.** prone to / reluctant to stay. They feel that predictions about earthquakes are not **9.** convinced / reliable, and we can never know when the next one will strike.

B | Using Vocabulary. Answer the questions. Share your ideas with a partner.

1. What weather signs are **indicative** of an approaching storm?
2. **Approximately** how often does your area have strong rainstorms?
3. Where do you look for weather updates? What do you think is the most **reliable** source of information?

> **Word Link**
> vict, vinc = conquering:
> **vict**ory, con**vince**, in**vinc**ible

C | Brainstorming. Discuss your answers to these questions in small groups.

1. Where do most people in your country live? In cities? Near water? Near mountains? Why do you think they live there?
2. How do volcanoes affect the lives of people who live near them?

D | Predicting. Look at the photos and read the title and headings in the reading passage on pages 73–75. What do you think the reading is about? Circle your answer and check your prediction as you read.

a. how to minimize the damage caused by earthquakes
b. why the risk of damage from natural disasters is increasing
c. where most natural disasters happen and how to predict them

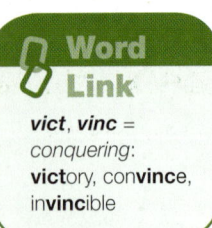

READING

Coping in a World of Risk

▲ Over the past decade, Australia's rural farming communities, including Balranald, New South Wales, have been affected by drought.

A For decades, scientists have been researching ways to predict natural disasters. Reliable methods of prediction could save hundreds — or sometimes thousands — of lives. However, despite researching various early warning signs that might indicate impending¹ disasters, scientists have not generally been successful at making reliable predictions. Some experts and governments have come to the conclusion that if natural disasters cannot be reliably predicted, then anticipation and preparation are the best defenses we have.

IS RISK ON THE RISE?

B Most scientists acknowledge that the risk of earthquakes, volcanic eruptions, hurricanes, floods, and drought is increasing, partly as a result of global warming. While they are reluctant to point to specific natural events as being caused by climate change, most scientists agree that the consequences of global warming will likely continue to have a significant impact on the number and the severity of natural disasters.

C Take, for example, the drought that has struck Australia for more than a decade. This calamitous² dry spell has destroyed orchards,³ livestock, and many of the nation's rice farms. Climatologists⁴ say this damage and destruction fits the pattern they expect from global warming. The same is true in Bangladesh, where people have been coping with the opposite problem—flooding. Two-thirds of this country of 150 million people is less than 17 feet (5 meters) above sea level. Climatologists say that by 2050, approximately one-fifth of the land could be under water due to rising sea levels, driving millions inland to already crowded cities.

---

¹ An **impending** event is one that is going to happen very soon.
² If an event is **calamitous**, it causes a great deal of damage or distress.
³ An **orchard** is an area of land on which fruit trees are grown.
⁴ A **climatologist** is a person who studies climates, or weather and its effects.

DANGER ZONES | 73

D In the past 15 years, there has also been an increase in the number of hurricanes hitting the U.S. coast. Experts predict that this increase will continue. "We expect the number of strikes over the next five years to be about 30 percent higher than the long-term historical average," says Robert Muir-Wood of Risk Management Solutions, a company that advises insurance companies.

E Some of the increased risk comes as the result of human behavior, such as increased human migration to high-risk areas. "Whether by choice, chance, or mistake, more of us have been moving into hazard-prone regions," says Brendan Meade, a geophysicist[5] at Harvard University. One-third of the world's population currently lives within 60 miles (100 kilometers) of the coast, where people face greater risks from tsunamis and hurricanes. Other people settle in earthquake zones, or live dangerously close to volcanoes. Still others live near rivers that are prone to flooding during heavy rains.

F Why do so many people choose to live in these high-risk areas? One reason is that farmers prefer the fertile lands of river deltas and volcanic slopes. Another likely factor is that workers in industrial countries find more jobs in coastal cities, where trade and international commerce thrive. People also sometimes choose to live near rivers, mountains, and beaches for their scenic beauty, and because of the many opportunities for outdoor activities.

TAKING ACTION TO REDUCE RISK

G Whatever the causes of the increased risk may be, the costs of disasters keep growing. Disaster-related risks are nine times higher than they were in the 1960s. Many nations are therefore taking action to protect their populations. In the Netherlands, for example, architects have designed floating houses that rise and fall with the changing water level in rivers. In the United Kingdom, government officials are strengthening flood-control barriers on London's River Thames. Chicago, Shanghai, and other cities are using green rooftops to reduce the effects of urban heat islands.[6] Considering the uncertainties of climate change and the difficulties of prediction, nations around the world are taking steps to get ready before the next disaster strikes.

THE PROBLEM OF PREDICTION

H In March 2009, a laboratory technician named Gioacchino Giuliani believed that a big earthquake would soon strike the Abruzzo region of central Italy. Giuliani warned that an increased concentration of radon gas in the area, along with tremors over previous months, were indicative of a coming earthquake near the town of L'Aquila. A week after his prediction, a 6.3-magnitude earthquake hit L'Aquila. Some 300 people were killed, and tens of thousands were injured or made homeless.

I Had Giuliani predicted the earthquake? Most scientists were not convinced. This was the third time Giuliani had warned of an impending earthquake based on similar evidence, and the previous two times he had been wrong. After the L'Aquila disaster, the Italian government asked U.S. seismologist[7] Thomas Jordan to lead an international commission to determine whether earthquakes were predictable. The commission's answer was an emphatic no. "It would be fantastic and exciting if we were able to predict the time and place of damaging earthquakes," says Michael Blanpied, a member of the National Earthquake Prediction Evaluation Council, "but so far we've had no success with specific predictions."

J Seismologist Susan Hough agrees. "The public would like scientists to predict earthquakes," she says, "[but] we can't do that. We might never be able to do that." As with other natural disasters, earthquake preparedness might be our best defense, for example, by doing things such as upgrading existing buildings, building stronger new buildings, and educating citizens about what to do in the event of a disaster. In this way, says Hough, we "can stop worrying about predicting the unpredictable and start doing more to prepare for the inevitable."

Update: On October 22, 2012, six Italian scientists and a government official were sentenced to six years in prison for giving "incomplete, imprecise, and contradictory" information before the 2009 L'Aquila earthquake. They plan to appeal the conviction.

---

[5] A **geophysicist** is a person who studies the Earth's physical properties and processes.

[6] The **urban heat island** effect refers to the way cities with concrete and brick buildings and streets absorb the sun's energy and heat the air, increasing the temperature around them.

[7] A **seismologist** is a scientist who studies earthquakes.

A truck crushed by a collapsed building reveals the devastating power of the 2010 Haiti earthquake. ▼

DANGER ZONES | 75

LESSON A — UNDERSTANDING THE READING

A | Identifying Main Ideas. Write the paragraph letter from the reading on pages 73–75 that best matches each main idea.

- _G_ 1. The cost of disasters is growing, and some countries are finding ways to protect their citizens.
- _J_ 2. Because we can't predict earthquakes, the best thing we can do is prepare ourselves.
- _B_ 3. There is evidence that global warming is causing severe droughts and flooding.
- _E_ 4. People choose to move to high-risk areas for various reasons.
- _E_ 5. More people are moving to hazard-prone areas, which is increasing risk.

B | Identifying Key Details: Scanning for Numbers. What does each number from the reading represent? Match each number to the correct information.

- _d_ 1. 150 million
- _g_ 2. 2050
- _e_ 3. 30 percent
- _b_ 4. 60
- _c_ 5. 2009
- _a_ 6. 6.3
- _f_ 7. 300

a. the magnitude of the earthquake that hit L'Aquila
b. the distance, in miles, that one-third of the world's population lives from the coast
c. the year that an Italian man predicted an earthquake would strike Abruzzo
d. the population of Bangladesh
e. how much higher the average number of hurricanes hitting the U.S. coast will be in the next five years
f. the number of people who were killed in the L'Aquila earthquake
g. the year by which one-fifth of Bangladesh might be under water

C | Identifying Reasons. Complete the chart with information from the reading.

High-risk Area	Why It's Dangerous (Type of Risk)	Why People Live There
Near the coast	tsunamis and hurricanes	Find more jobs, trade
Close to volcanoes	earthquake zones	the fertile lands.
Near rivers	flooding because of heavy rains	opportunities for outdoor activities

D | Critical Thinking: Analyzing Evidence. Find at least one fact and at least one quote from an expert that supports each claim below from the reading. For each quote, include the name of the speaker. Then discuss with a partner: Does the evidence for each claim seem convincing? Why or why not?

Claim	The risk of natural disasters is increasing.	Earthquakes cannot be predicted.
Fact		
Quote		

CT Focus

Writers often provide details or examples as **evidence** to prove or support a claim made in an article. Evidence can be provided as a factual statement or as a quote from an expert in the field.

DEVELOPING READING SKILLS

Reading Skill: Organizing Your Notes

Taking notes on a long reading passage can help you to:

- understand the passage (it helps you to pay attention to the most important ideas).
- memorize and organize key facts more easily.
- recall and use the information at a later time, for example, in an essay or an exam.

You probably take notes in the margins of a text, or highlight or underline key points as you read. After you've finished reading, however, you can organize your notes in a graphic organizer. For example, if the reading passage describes a process or a sequence of events, you can organize your notes in an outline or on a time line. If the reading passage compares two things, you can write notes in a T-chart or a Venn diagram. If the passage, or a section of a passage, describes information related to a main idea, you can organize your notes using a concept map.

Remember to leave out repeated information and any unnecessary words to make your notes as brief as possible.

For more information about note-taking, see page 242.

A | Categorizing Information. Complete this concept map using information from "Taking Action to Reduce Risk" on page 74.

Problem: Increase in disaster-related risks

Why?

Solutions: Nations are _____ .

Examples

Where?

_____ _____ cities such as _____ _____

How?

floating _____ _____ _____
_____ _____ _____
_____ _____ _____

B | Sequencing Information. On a separate piece of paper, create a timeline to note the sequence of events described in the section "The Problem Of Prediction" on page 74.

VIEWING

Hurricanes

Before Viewing

▲ Hurricane winds hit downtown Miami, Florida, during Hurricane Wilma, one of the most intense tropical cyclones ever recorded in the Atlantic.

A | Using a Dictionary. Here are some words you will hear in the video. Match each word with the correct definition. Use your dictionary to help you.

3 atomic bomb	5 hallmark	4 sensor	1 tropical	2 warning
nuclear bomb	*sign*			*caution*

1. _____: from an area of the world that is characterized by a hot climate
2. _____: a hint of danger
3. _____: a nuclear weapon that releases an enormous amount of energy
4. _____: a device that can notice and measure signals or changes
5. _____: a characteristic or feature of something

B | Thinking Ahead. How do hurricanes form? Number the sentences in order (1–7). Share your ideas with a partner. Then check your predictions as you view the video.

- _5_ The storm becomes a hurricane when winds reach 74 miles per hour.
- _7_ Dry air blowing downward in the center creates a calm area called the eye.
- _2_ Warm, moist air above these areas form thunderstorms.
- _4_ When the winds are faster than 39 miles per hour, it is called a tropical storm.
- _1_ The sun heats large areas of tropical ocean to more than 82 degrees Fahrenheit.
- _3_ Winds form a circular pattern of clouds called a tropical depression.
- _6_ In the eye wall, bands of rain and winds of up to 200 miles an hour spiral upward.

While Viewing

Read questions 1–3. Think about the answers as you view the video.

1. What are two other words for "hurricane"?
2. How much energy does a hurricane release in one day?
3. In what seasons of the year do hurricanes form?

After Viewing

A | Discuss your answers to questions (1–3) above with a partner.

B | Critical Thinking. What is one thing that hurricanes and earthquakes have in common? What is one way they are different?

78 | UNIT 4

PREPARING TO READ

LESSON B

A | Building Vocabulary. Find the words in **blue** in the reading passage on pages 80–84. Use the context to guess their meanings. Then match the sentence parts below to make definitions.

1. When you **accumulate** things, __d__
2. If something **collapses**, __e__
3. If something is **compacted**, __h__
4. A **crack** is __i__
5. An **eruption** is an event when __b__
6. If an object **explodes**, __f__
7. You use **extraordinary** (remarkable, very unusually) to describe __c__
8. The **pressure** in a place or container is __j__
9. The **range** of something is __a__
10. If something **tends to** occur, __g__

a. the maximum area it can reach.
b. a volcano throws out hot rock, ash, and steam.
c. something or someone that has extremely good or special qualities.
d. you collect or gather them over a period of time.
e. it falls down suddenly.
f. it bursts with great force.
g. it usually happens or it often happens.
h. it is densely packed or pressed together as a result of external pressure.
i. a line that appears on the surface of something when it is slightly damaged.
j. the force produced in that space by a quantity of gas or liquid.

B | Using Vocabulary. Answer the questions in complete sentences. Then share your sentences with a partner.

1. What kinds of things have you **accumulated** in your home?
2. What type of music do you **tend to** listen to most?
3. Name someone you think is **extraordinary**. Explain your answer.

C | Brainstorming. What do you know about volcanoes? How do you think a "supervolcano" might be different from other volcanoes? Discuss your ideas in a small group.

_____

_____

> **Word Partners**
> Use **tend to** with verbs: tend to **agree**, tend to **avoid**, tend to **feel**, tend to **forget**, tend to **happen**, tend to **think**, and with nouns: **people** tend to, **children/men/women** tend to.

D | Predicting. Read the title and the three headings in the reading passage on pages 80–84.

1. How is the information presented? Circle all that apply.

   explanatory text   infographics   pie chart   map   time line   Venn diagram

2. What do you think the reading explains? As you read, check your prediction(s).

   a. how a specific supervolcano in the USA was formed
   b. how to protect yourself from a supervolcano
   c. how a supervolcano can affect large parts of the world

Yellowstone's Smoking Bomb

A YELLOWSTONE NATIONAL PARK, the oldest and most famous national park in the United States, sits on top of one of the biggest volcanoes on Earth. Yellowstone's volcano is so big that many scientists call it a *supervolcano*. As the name suggests, supervolcanoes are much bigger and more powerful than ordinary volcanoes, and their eruptions can be exceptionally violent and destructive. When volcanoes erupt, they can kill plants and animals for miles around. When a supervolcano explodes, it can threaten whole species with extinction by changing the climate across the entire planet.

What Causes a Supervolcano to Erupt?

B No supervolcano has erupted in recorded human history. However, in the 2.1 million years that Yellowstone has sat over the supervolcano, scientists believe that the park has experienced three super-eruptions. Geologists who study Yellowstone's supervolcano have pieced together the sequence of events that probably cause a super-eruption. First, an intense plume of heat pushes up from deep within the Earth. The extreme heat melts rock and creates a huge chamber a few miles below the surface. The chamber slowly fills with a pressurized mix of magma (melted rock), water vapor, carbon dioxide, and other gases. As additional magma accumulates in the chamber over thousands of years, the land on the surface above it begins to move up to form a dome, inches at a time. As the dome moves higher, cracks form along its edges. When the pressure in the magma chamber is released through the cracks in the dome, the gases suddenly explode, creating a violent super-eruption and emptying the magma chamber. Once the magma chamber is empty, the dome collapses, leaving a giant *caldera*, or crater, in the ground. Yellowstone's caldera, which covers a 25- by 37-mile (or 40- by 60-kilometer) area in the state of Wyoming, was formed after the last super-eruption some 640,000 years ago.

(continued on page 84)

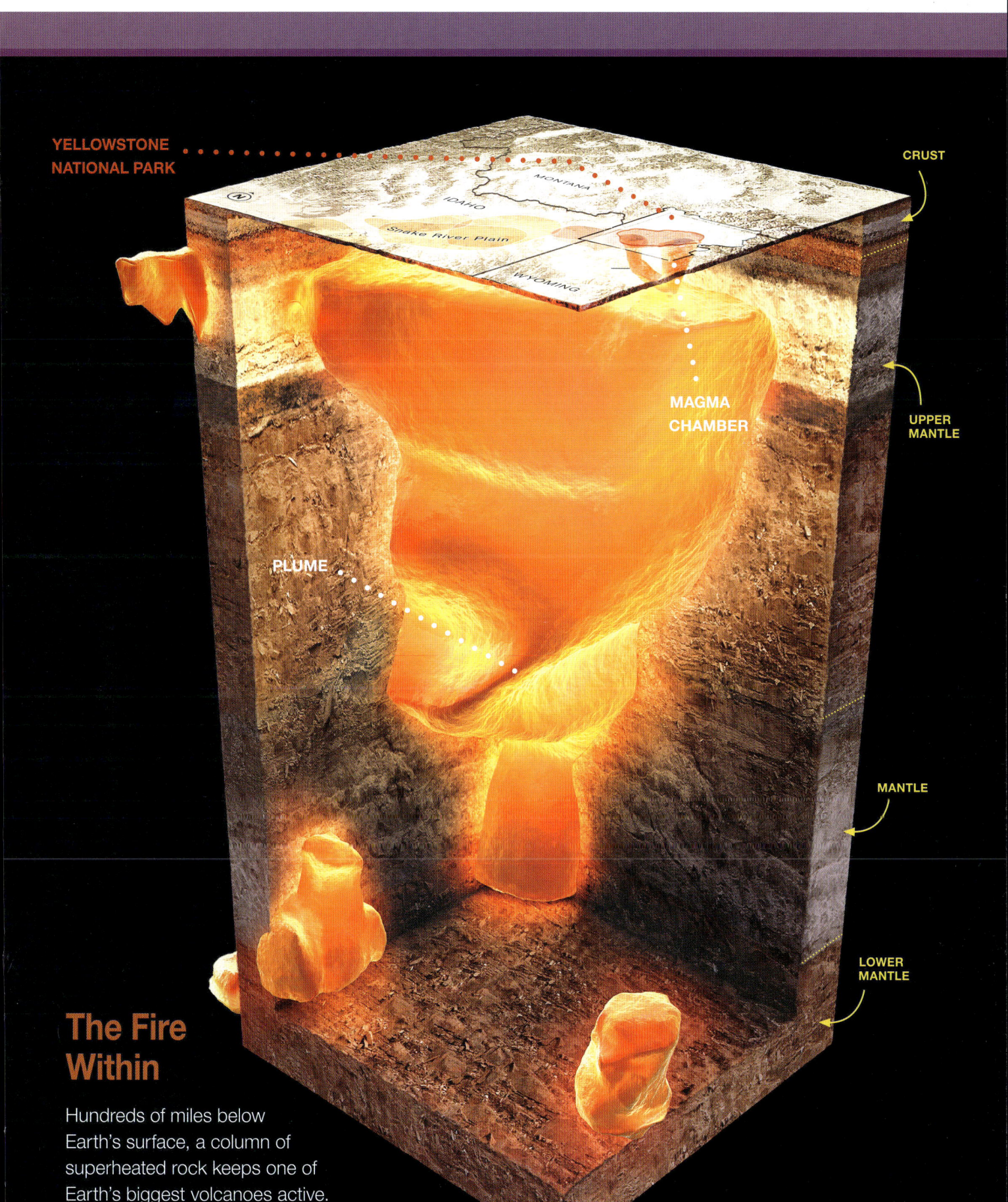

YELLOWSTONE NATIONAL PARK

CRUST

MAGMA CHAMBER

UPPER MANTLE

PLUME

MANTLE

LOWER MANTLE

The Fire Within

Hundreds of miles below Earth's surface, a column of superheated rock keeps one of Earth's biggest volcanoes active.

LESSON B — READING

A Waking Giant?

1870: Army officer Gustavus Doane explores the region that will later become Yellowstone National Park. He notices there is a huge open space, or basin, surrounded by mountains, and concludes that it is the crater of a huge extinct volcano.

1950s: Harvard graduate student Francis Boyd discovers a thick layer of heated and compacted ash at Yellowstone, and determines that it is the result of a geologically recent eruption.

1970s: Supervolcano expert Bob Smith of the University of Utah finds that land near the caldera has risen by some 30 inches (76 centimeters) in three decades, proving the supervolcano is alive.

1985: A number of small earthquakes strike the area, causing the land to sink. Over the next decade, it sinks eight inches (20 centimeters).

2004–2007: The ground above the caldera rises upward at rates as high as 2.8 inches (7 centimeters) a year—much faster than any uplift since observations began in the 1970s.

2007–2010: The ground rise slows to one centimeter or less a year, but the ground has risen about 10 inches (25 centimeters) in just a few years. "It's an extraordinary uplift," says Smith, "because it covers such a large area and the rates are so high."

▲ Fire and debris rise from deep within the Earth under Yellowstone in this artist's view of a supervolcanic eruption.

DANGER ZONES | 83

How Violent Is a Super-Eruption?

After each super-eruption at Yellowstone, the whole planet felt the effects. Scientists theorize that gases rising high into the atmosphere mixed with water vapor to create a haze that reduced sunlight, causing a period of cooling across the globe. It is estimated that the combined debris[1] from the three eruptions was so vast it could have filled the Grand Canyon.

The most recent catastrophic eruption, about 640,000 years ago, poured out 240 cubic miles (1,000 cubic kilometers) of rock, lava, and ash. A column of ash rose some 100,000 feet (30 kilometers) into the atmosphere, and winds carried ash and dust across the western half of the United States and south to the Gulf of Mexico. Closer to the supervolcano, thick clouds of ash, rocks, and gas—superheated to 1,470 F° (800 C°)—rolled over the land. This volcano's lava and debris destroyed everything within its devastating range, filling entire valleys and forming layers hundreds of feet thick.

Will the Supervolcano Erupt Again?

Predicting when an eruption might occur is extremely difficult, in part because scientists still do not understand all the details of what is happening under the caldera's surface. Moreover, they have kept continuous records of Yellowstone's activity only since the 1970s—a tiny slice of geologic time—making it hard to draw conclusions. However, scientists theorize that Yellowstone's magma chamber expands periodically from a plume of hot rock moving up from deep inside the Earth. As the chamber expands, it pushes the land above it upward. According to this theory, when the plume of rock decreases, the magma cools and becomes solid, allowing the land above to fall back.

Scientists believe that Yellowstone has probably seen a continuous cycle of rising and falling land over the past 15,000 years. Geophysicist and supervolcano expert Bob Smith of the University of Utah believes the rise-and-fall cycle of Yellowstone's caldera will likely continue. "These calderas tend to go up and down, up and down," he says. "We call this a caldera at unrest. The net effect over many cycles is to finally get enough magma to erupt. And we don't know what those cycles are."

So, is the supervolcano going to explode again? Some kind of eruption is highly likely at some point. The chances of another catastrophic super-eruption are anyone's guess. It could happen in this century, or 100,000 years from now. No one knows for sure.

The Yellowstone Eruptions

Three major blasts have shaken Yellowstone National Park during the past 2 million years. The smallest of these, 1.3 million years ago, produced 280 times more material than the 1980 eruption of Mount St. Helens. After the two biggest eruptions, winds carried material from Yellowstone across much of the United States.

Comparative Volume of Eruptions
in cubic miles

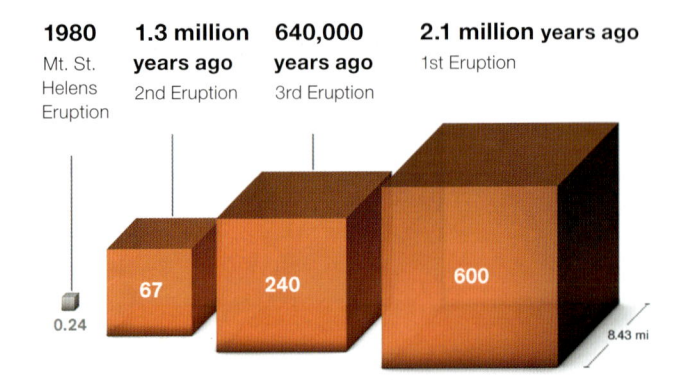

1980 Mt. St. Helens Eruption	1.3 million years ago 2nd Eruption	640,000 years ago 3rd Eruption	2.1 million years ago 1st Eruption
0.24	67	240	600 (8.43 mi)

Ash Coverages

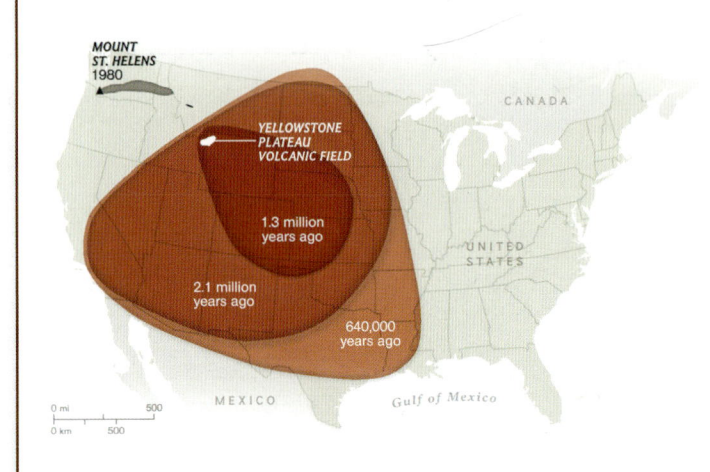

[1] **Debris** is pieces from something that has been destroyed, or pieces of trash or unwanted material that are spread around.

UNDERSTANDING THE READING

A | Identifying Main Ideas. Complete the main ideas of the paragraphs listed below.

1. Paragraph E: It's _extremely difficult_ to predict a supervolcano _eruption_, but scientists are beginning to understand how a supervolcano changes over time.

2. Paragraph F: Scientists think that Yellowstone has experienced a cycle of _rising_ and _falling land_ for 15,000 years.

3. Paragraph G: _No one_ knows when the supervolcano will erupt again, but it probably _going to_ erupt again sometime in the future.

B | Identifying Meaning from Context. Find and underline the following words in the reading passage on pages 80–84. Use context to help you complete the definitions. Check your answers in a dictionary.

1. Paragraph A: You use **exceptionally** to describe something that is true to a (very large / very slight) degree.

2. Paragraph C: **Haze** is a light mist caused by particles of water or dust (on the ground / in the atmosphere).

3. Paragraph D: **Catastrophic** means extremely (destructive / impressive).

4. Paragraph F: The **net effect** of something is the effect (before / after) all the details have been considered or included.

C | Identifying Key Details. Find details in the reading passage and the graphics to answer the following questions.

1. What is the difference between a volcano and a supervolcano?
   A supervolcano is much bigger and more powerful than ordinary volcano.

2. According to scientists, how many times has the Yellowstone supervolcano erupted in the last 2.1 million years?
   3 supereruptions

3. How and when was the Yellowstone caldera formed?
   _____

4. Why is it difficult for scientists to predict when the supervolcano will erupt again? Give two reasons.
   1st: scientists still don't understand all the details of what is happening under the caldera's surface.
   2nd: They kept records of Yellowstone's act only since 1970s - tiny slice of geologic line → hard to draw conclusions

LESSON B — UNDERSTANDING THE READING

D | Understanding Infographics. Use the information on page 84 to answer the questions.

1. When did Yellowstone produce the greatest amount of material in an eruption?

   2.1 million years ago

2. When did ash from a Yellowstone eruption cover about half of the United States?

   640,000 years ago

E | Labeling a Process Diagram. Label the illustrations (a–f) to show the sequence of events in a supervolcano eruption.

a. After weeks or months, the chamber becomes empty.

b. A plume of extreme heat rises from deep within the Earth.

c. Columns of ash may rise 25 miles (40 kilometers) into the air.

d. Pressure forces gases to explode upward through cracks in the dome.

e. The chamber pushes the surface of the land to form a dome.

f. The intense heat melts rock, creating a chamber just below the surface.

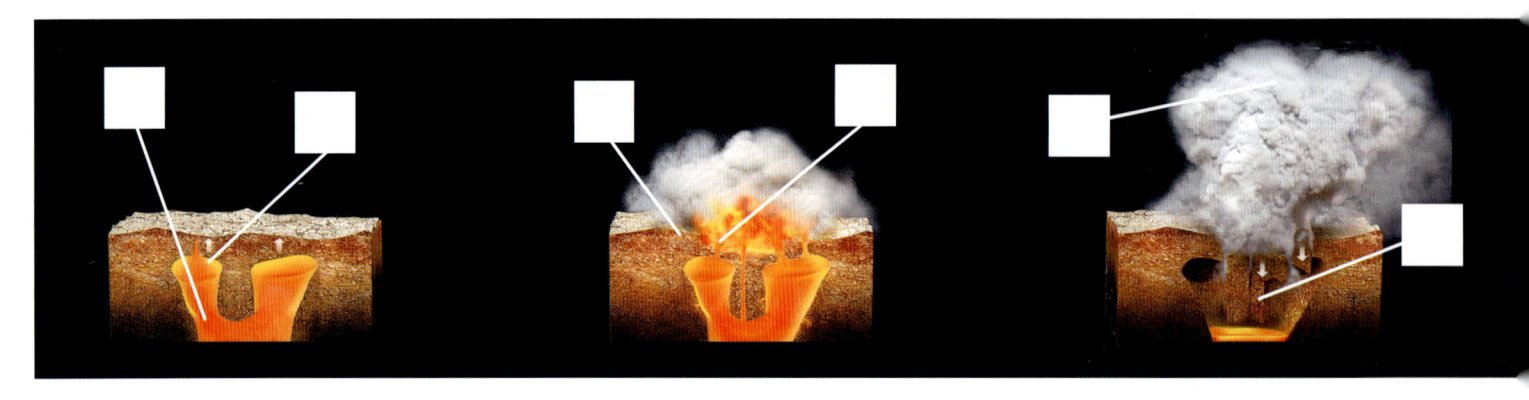

Before the Eruption   **The Volcano Erupts**   **After the Eruption**

F | Critical Thinking: Analyzing Evidence. Look at the time line on page 82 and answer the questions.

1. List two pieces of evidence that show there has been a large eruption at Yellowstone.

2. What evidence shows that the supervolcano is still alive?

G | Critical Thinking: Synthesizing. What do earthquakes and the Yellowstone supervolcano have in common? Discuss ideas in a small group.

EXPLORING WRITTEN ENGLISH

LESSON C

GOAL: Writing Opinion Paragraphs
In this lesson, you are going to plan, write, revise, and edit paragraphs on the following topic: **Choose one type of natural disaster. Write about one way that individuals can prepare for it and one way that governments prepare for it.**

A | Brainstorming. Make a list of natural disasters. For each natural disaster, list the type of damage it can cause.

Natural Disaster	Damage It Can Cause
earthquakes	buildings fall

Free Writing. Think about the dangers caused by one of the natural disasters in your list. How can people prepare for this type of disaster? Write for five minutes.

B | Read the information in the box. Then complete the sentences (1–5) with parallel structures.

Language for Writing: Using parallel structures

When you join two ideas in one sentence, both ideas have to be in the same form. For example, the words and phrases before and after *and* must both be nouns, adjectives, or verbs (in the same tense). Also, the two parallel ideas should come immediately before and after *and*.

Parallel nouns:
Property gets damaged in earthquakes. / Earthquakes damage buildings.
Property and **buildings** get damaged in earthquakes.

Parallel verbs:
Learn about earthquake safety online. / Phone numbers for local shelters are online.
You can **learn** about earthquake safety and **find** phone numbers for local shelters online.

Parallel adjectives:
The people were hungry. They also needed to sleep. → The people were **hungry** and **tired**.

1. People can prepare for a hurricane by buying extra water. They also need extra food.

   People can prepare for a hurricane by buying extra _____ and _____.

2. When it starts to rain, streets will be slippery. Slippery streets can be dangerous.

   When it starts to rain, streets will be _____ and _____.

3. People need to be cautious. People aren't aware of dangers.

   People need to be _____ and _____ of dangers.

DANGER ZONES | 87

LESSON C   EXPLORING WRITTEN ENGLISH

4. Houses were crushed. The tornado carried cars away.

   The tornado _____ houses and _____ cars away.

5. People are frightened of hurricanes. Hurricanes cause damage to property.

   Hurricanes _____ people and _____ property.

> **Writing Skill:** Writing an Introductory Paragraph
>
> The first paragraph of an essay is the **introductory paragraph**. This paragraph contains the thesis statement and general information about the essay. It can also include an engaging opening to make the reader interested. For example, it can start with a surprising statement or an interesting question. See the first sentence on page 80 for an example.
>
> In an introduction, you should generally avoid using *I*, unless it is a personal essay. For example, you should avoid saying, *I am going to write about . . .*

C | **Critical Thinking: Analyzing.** Read the introductory paragraphs below and discuss these questions with a partner.

1. Where is the thesis statement? Underline it.
2. According to the thesis statement, what is the essay going to be about?
3. Is there an engaging opening, such as an interesting statement or question?
4. Which introduction do you think is better? Why?

Paragraph A

Most people may not realize it, but your home can be a very dangerous place. Accidents at home are the leading cause of death in some countries. Children and the elderly are the most likely people to hurt themselves or die due to home accidents. Some of the most common accidents at home are falls, poisoning, fire, choking, and drowning. Fortunately, however, there are a few things you can do to make your house a safe place for you and your family.

Paragraph B

There are things you can do to make your house a safe place for you and your family. Accidents at home are a common and frequent cause of injury and death. Children and the elderly are the most likely people to hurt themselves or die due to home accidents. Some of the most common accidents at home are falls, poisoning, fire, choking, and drowning. In this essay, I'm going to provide some ways to protect yourself from home accidents.

WRITING TASK: Drafting

A | Planning. Follow the steps to make notes for your paragraphs.

Step 1 Write the type of natural disaster you are going to discuss in the outline below and complete the thesis statement.

Step 2 Think about an interesting or surprising statement or question to open your introductory paragraph. Write it in the outline.

Step 3 Decide the two best ways people can prepare for the type of disaster you've chosen. Write topic sentences for each of your body paragraphs.

Step 4 Now write two or three examples or details for each body paragraph, for example, why this kind of preparation is useful, how it can be done, what kind of damage or harm it might prevent.

B | Draft 1. Use your outline to write a first draft of your paragraph.

Introductory Paragraph

Natural Disaster: _____

Thesis statement: In order to be prepared for _____ , people need to
                                              disaster

_____ and governments need to _____ .
   first way   *second way*

Opening statement or question:

_____

_____

Body Paragraph 1: Topic sentence: One thing people can do to prepare is _____

_____ .
                    first way

Example/detail 1: _____

Example/detail 2: _____

Example/detail 3: _____

Body Paragraph 2: Topic sentence: One thing governments can do to prepare is _____

_____ .
                    second way

Example/detail 1: _____

Example/detail 2: _____

Example/detail 3: _____

LESSON C WRITING TASK: Revising

C | Critical Thinking: Analyzing. Work with a partner. Read the paragraphs about ways to prepare for an emergency while traveling. Then follow the steps to analyze the paragraphs.

When most people plan a vacation, they tend to spend a lot of time choosing a hotel, finding a good flight, and deciding what sites they want to see, but they may not plan for possible travel emergencies. A little bit of planning ahead of time, however, can save travelers a lot of problems later. It's particularly important to be prepared for medical emergencies and theft. In order to be prepared for an emergency, travelers should think about their medical needs, and also consider what they might need in case of the theft or loss of important items.

Thinking about their medical needs beforehand can save travelers a lot of time and trouble. They should pack enough medication to last for the whole trip so they don't have to refill prescriptions while they're traveling. They should also keep their prescription medications in the original bottles, so that if they do have to refill a prescription for some reason, they will know the name of the medication and the dosage. In addition, travelers should pack a first-aid kit containing bandages, pain relievers, antibiotic creams, and any other necessary items.

People should also consider what they might need in case of the theft or loss of items such as passports and credit cards. It's a good idea for travelers to know the phone numbers of their embassies or consulates in case their passports are stolen. Travelers should also leave copies of their passports with friends or family members at home, and they should also keep copies in different parts of their luggage. This way it will be easier to get replacement passports if necessary. Finally, people who are traveling should know the phone numbers of their credit card companies so they can cancel their cards immediately after they are lost or stolen.

Step 1 Circle the opening statement or question.

Step 2 Underline the thesis statement in the introductory paragraph.

Step 3 Underline the topic sentences in the two body paragraphs.

Step 4 Circle the key words in each topic sentence that match the key words in the thesis statement.

Step 5 In the first body paragraph, check (✓) sentences that explain how or why travelers should think of medical needs.

Step 6 In the second body paragraph, check (✓) sentences that explain how or why travelers should consider what they might need in case of loss or theft.

D | Revising. Follow steps 1–6 in exercise **C** to analyze your own paragraphs.

E | Peer Evaluation. Exchange your first draft with a partner and follow the steps below.

Step 1 Read your partner's paragraphs and tell him or her one thing that you liked about them.

Step 2 Complete the outline below showing the ideas that your partner's paragraphs describe.

Introductory Paragraph

Natural Disaster: _____

Thesis statement: In order to be prepared for _____, people need to
                                                    disaster

_____ and governments need to _____.
      first way   *second way*

Opening statement or question:

_____

_____

Body Paragraph 1: Topic sentence: One thing people can do to prepare is _____

_____.
                              first way

Example/detail 1: _____

Example/detail 2: _____

Example/detail 3: _____

Body Paragraph 2: Topic sentence: One thing governments can do to prepare is _____

_____.
                              second way

Example/detail 1: _____

Example/detail 2: _____

Example/detail 3: _____

Step 3 Compare this outline with the one that your partner created in exercise **B** on page 89.

Step 4 The two outlines should be similar. If they aren't, discuss how they differ.

LESSON C — WRITING TASK: Editing

F | Draft 2. Write a second draft of your paragraphs. Use what you learned from the peer evaluation activity and your answers to exercise **D**. Make any other necessary changes.

G | Editing Practice. Read the information in the box. Then find and correct one mistake with parallel structures in each of the sentences (1–5).

> In sentences with parallel structure, remember:
> - both ideas have to be in the same form, so when combining sentences you may have to shift words around, change a verb tense, or change a verb to an adjective.
> - the two parallel ideas should come immediately before and after *and*.

1. People can prepare for fires by creating an escape plan and discuss the plan with family members.

2. Keep important papers and putting medicine in one place.

3. If you will need to take pets with you, pet carriers are important to have and extra pet food.

4. Walk around your house and to identify things you will need to take.

5. Pack a bag with clothes for each family member and necessities.

H | Editing Checklist. Use the checklist to find errors in your second draft.

Editing Checklist	Yes	No
1. Are all the words spelled correctly?		
2. Is the first word of every sentence capitalized?		
3. Does every sentence end with the correct punctuation?		
4. Do your subjects and verbs agree?		
5. Did you use parallel structure correctly?		
6. Are verb tenses correct?		

I | Final Draft. Now use your Editing Checklist to write a third draft of your paragraphs. Make any other necessary changes.

UNIT 5

The Business of Tourism

ACADEMIC PATHWAYS

Lesson A: Analyzing causes and effects argument
Analyzing a writer's argument
Lesson B: Reading related travel news reports
Lesson C: Writing well developed body paragraphs
Writing a short cause-effect essay

Think and Discuss

1. What benefits can tourism bring to a region or a country?
2. What problems can tourism cause?

Tourists crowd the grounds at the Taj Mahal, in Agra, India. ▲

Exploring the Theme

Read the information, study the map and chart, and discuss the questions.

1. Which country receives more international tourists than any other country? Why do you think this is?

2. Which parts of the world are experiencing fast growth in tourism? Which countries do you think will be the top tourist destinations ten years from now? How about 50 years?

3. How popular is your own country for international tourists? How does the tourism business affect your country?

Charting International Tourism

Tourism can be a significant contributor to a nation's economy. Europe is the world's top destination for international tourists. Many tourists in Europe are Europeans themselves, while others come largely from Asia and the Americas. France is the most popular destination for international tourists. The United States, the most popular destination in North America, generates more money through tourism than any other country. Other increasingly popular tourist destinations include China and South Africa.

Crowds of tourists gather to photograph Leonardo da Vinci's *Mona Lisa* ▶ at the Louvre, Paris. The Louvre is one of the top attractions in the world's most popular tourist destination.

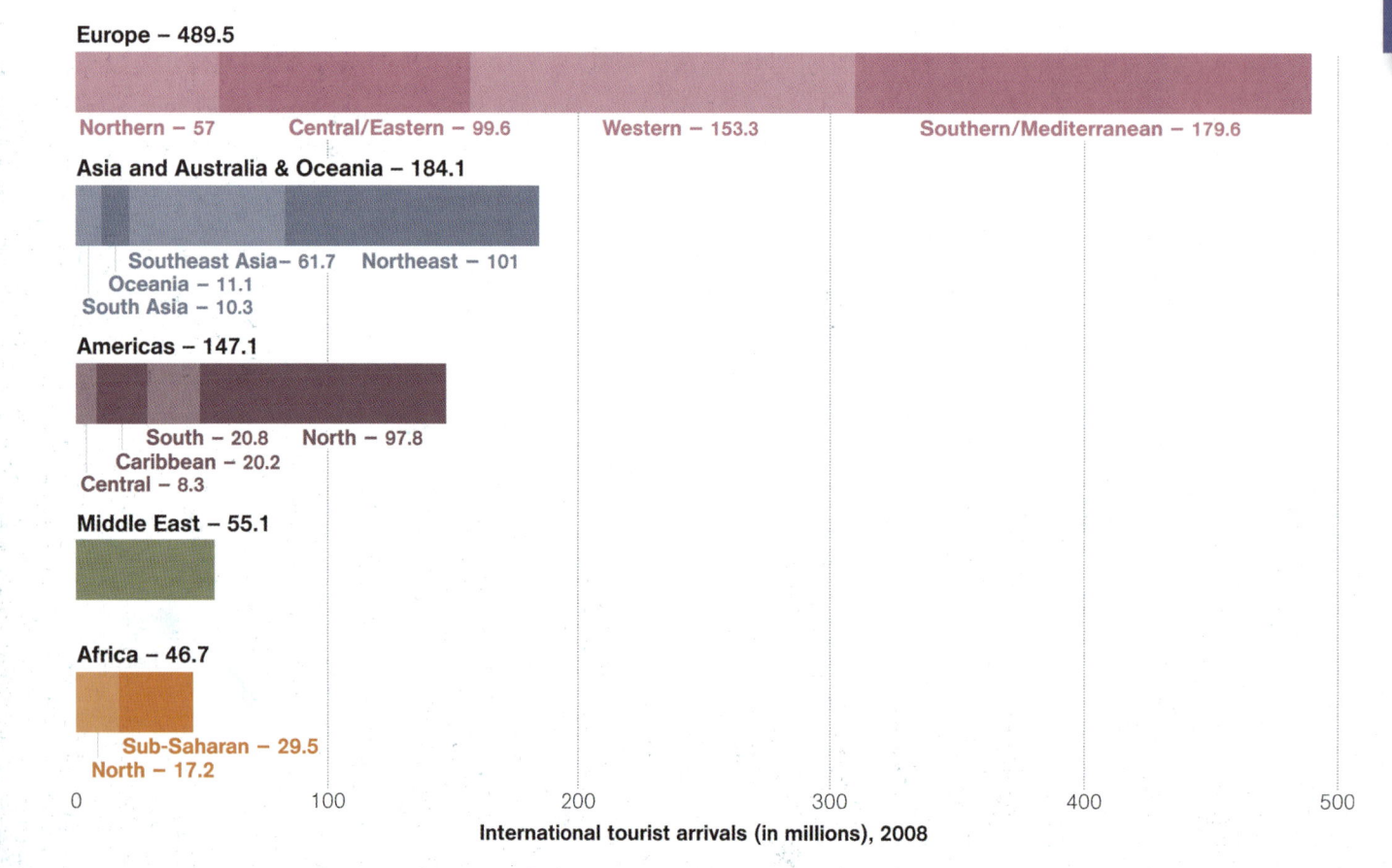

Europe – 489.5
- Northern – 57
- Central/Eastern – 99.6
- Western – 153.3
- Southern/Mediterranean – 179.6

Asia and Australia & Oceania – 184.1
- Southeast Asia – 61.7
- Northeast – 101
- Oceania – 11.1
- South Asia – 10.3

Americas – 147.1
- South – 20.8
- North – 97.8
- Caribbean – 20.2
- Central – 8.3

Middle East – 55.1

Africa – 46.7
- Sub-Saharan – 29.5
- North – 17.2

International tourist arrivals (in millions), 2008

International tourist arrivals
(in thousands per year)

- More than 40,000
- 4,001–40,000
- 401–4,000
- 100–400
- Less than 100
- No data

FRANCE
75,580

NORTH AMERICA
SOUTH AMERICA
EUROPE
AFRICA
ASIA
AUSTRALIA

©2005

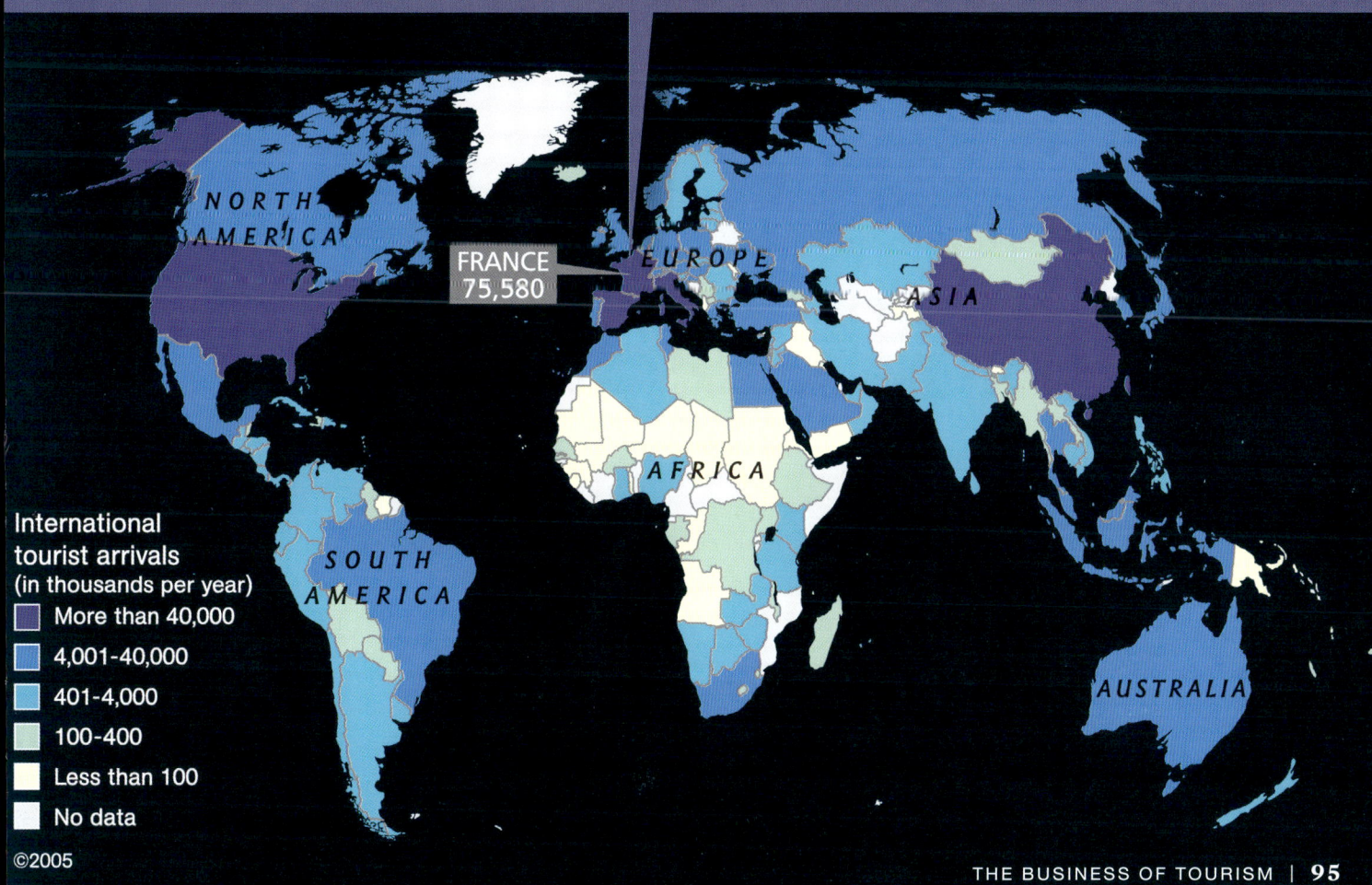

THE BUSINESS OF TOURISM | 95

LESSON A — PREPARING TO READ

A | Building Vocabulary. Find the words in **blue** in the reading passage on pages 97–99. Use the context to guess their meanings. Then write the correct word from the box to complete each sentence (1–10).

7 advocate	2 alternative	6 core	9 distinctive	1 enormous
5 expand	10 partnership	3 promote	8 scope	4 via

1. Something that is _____ is extremely large in size, amount, or degree.
2. A(n) _____ is another or different way of doing something.
3. If people _____ something, they encourage other people to use it.
4. If you do something _____ a particular means or person, you do it by way of or using that means or person.
5. If things _____, they become larger.
6. The _____ way of doing something is the main or most important way of doing it.
7. A(n) _____ of a particular action or plan is someone who recommends and supports it.
8. The _____ of an activity is the whole area that it deals with or includes.
9. Something that is _____ has a special quality or feature that makes it easily recognizable.
10. A(n) _____ is a relationship in which two or more people work together to accomplish something.

Word Link
mot = moving: pro**mot**e, **mot**ion, **mot**ivate

B | Using Vocabulary. Answer the questions. Share your ideas with a partner.

1. What are some **distinctive** travel destinations in your country or region?
2. Have you seen any ads or commercials that **promote** tourism in your country or region? If so, describe them.
3. Which countries in your part of the world are **expanding** their tourist industry?

C | Brainstorming. Discuss your answers to these questions in a small group.

1. Do you think people travel more now than in the past? Explain your answer.
2. What are some possible effects of large numbers of people visiting a natural area, such as a beach or a forest?
3. In your opinion, what is the best way to learn about a new place when you travel?

D | Predicting. Read the first paragraph on page 97. What do you think "geotourism" is? What solutions might it offer? Check your predictions as you read the rest of the passage.

READING

The New Face of Tourism

▲ An Arctic tourist snaps photos of a polar bear on pack ice near Svalbard, Norway.

A THE TWENTY-FIRST CENTURY has introduced a new era of mass tourism. By one estimate, over one billion international tourist trips were taken in 2010. With this tourism explosion comes the increased risk of endangering the distinctive places that make a destination unique and worth visiting. A new kind of tourism—geotourism—may offer a solution.

B Jonathan Tourtellot is founding director of the National Geographic Society's Center for Sustainable Destinations (CSD). The CSD's mission is to protect and maintain the world's distinctive places through wisely managed tourism. Tourtellot is an advocate of "geotourism," a term he came up with to describe the core strategy for achieving this goal. He believes that as mass tourism continues to increase and to expand into previously remote destinations, geotourism needs to be a long-term strategy. "The challenge of managing tourism in a way that protects places instead of overrunning[1] them," says Tourtellot, "is simply going to become larger."

C Geotourism provides an alternative to traditional mass tourism, the effects of which can be harmful to the local people as well as to the environment. Much of the infrastructure that supports mass tourism—large tourist hotels, restaurants, malls, tour companies—may be owned and operated by companies based outside the tourist areas. Chain restaurants[2] and stores may not always serve local food or sell local products. Large package tour[3] companies may not always hire local experts and guides, who know the area's history, environment, and culture. As a result, much of the money made from this type of tourism does not stay in the local community. Moreover, tourists whose only travel experience comes via big hotels, chain restaurants, or package tours typically have little contact with the local people, thus limiting their understanding of the nature and culture of the places they visit.

D In contrast, geotourism is like a partnership between travelers and locals. Geotravelers stay in locally owned hotels, managed by residents who care about protecting the area and environment. They eat in local restaurants serving regional cuisine. They buy from local merchants and craftspeople, hire local travel guides, and go to see traditional music, dance, and theater to broaden the scope of their understanding of the area's history and culture. Geotravelers learn a lot from their close contact with local people while the money they spend stays in the community, helps local people earn a living, and helps preserve and sustain the area for future travelers. In this way, geotourism benefits both partners—travelers and residents.

[1] If you **overrun** a place, you occupy it quickly.
[2] **Chain restaurants** are ones that have a similar appearance, serve similar food, and are all owned by the same company.
[3] A **package tour** is a vacation in which your travel and accommodation are booked for you.

THE BUSINESS OF TOURISM

LESSON A   READING

An interview with Jonathan Tourtellot, Geotourism Pioneer

Q. How would you differentiate among ecotourism, sustainable tourism, and geotourism?

Tourtellot: Ecotourism focuses specifically on natural areas. I'm convinced that there are elephants roaming Africa and trees growing in Costa Rica that would not be there without ecotourism. Sustainable tourism . . . seems to say, "Keep everything the way it is." We needed a term that would bring the ecotourism principle out of its niche[4] and cover everything that makes travel interesting. Geotourism is defined as tourism that sustains or enhances the geographical character of a place—the environment, heritage, aesthetics,[5] culture, and well-being of local people.

Q. What happens when tourism is badly managed?

Tourtellot: It can destroy a place. Coasts, for example, are extremely vulnerable. Coasts are important for biodiversity[6] because much of marine life has its nurseries[7] in coastline areas. So development there is a highly sensitive issue. Same thing goes for attractive mountainsides like the Rockies of the West. That's why when development occurs on a large scale, it's important that it be . . . well planned.

Q. What happens to a destination after years of heavy traffic?

Tourtellot: Here's an example—at the Petrified Forest [in northeast Arizona] it's very easy to bend down, pick up a little bit of petrified wood, and pocket it. People think it's only one pebble[8] in such a vast area, so it makes no difference if they take it. But since millions of visitors over the years have thought the same thing, all of the pebbles have disappeared—meaning there's been an enormous loss of what makes the Petrified Forest so special. So, when you're talking about an entire location like a town, a stretch of coastline, a wild area, or a national park, it's important to listen to park rangers when they tell you where to go and not go, what to do and not do.

▲ Nearly two million tourists a year come to Monument Valley, on the U.S. state border between Arizona and Utah.

Q. What happens when tourism is managed well?

Tourtellot: It can save a place. When people come see something special and unique to an area—its nature, historic structures, great cultural events, beautiful landscapes, even special cuisine—they are enjoying and learning more about a destination's geographical character . . . [T]ravelers spend their money in a way that helps maintain the geographical diversity and distinctiveness of the place they're visiting. It can be as simple as spending your money at a little restaurant that serves a regional dish, with ingredients from local farmers, rather than at an international franchise[9] that serves the same food you can get back home.

[4] A **niche** is a special area of demand for a product or a service.
[5] **Aesthetics** relates to the appreciation and study of a beauty.
[6] **Biodiversity** is the existence of a wide variety of plants and animals living in their natural environment.
[7] Marine-life **nurseries** are places where young sea animals are cared for while they are growing.

Q. How else can tourism help benefit a destination?

Tourtellot: Great tourism can build something that wasn't there before. My favorite example is the Monterey Bay Aquarium in California. It was built in a restored cannery[10] building on historic Cannery Row—which is a good example of preserving a historical building rather than destroying it. The aquarium, which has about 1.8 million visitors each year, brought people's attention to the incredible variety of sea life right off the coast of California. And it played a major role in the development of the Monterey Bay National Marine Sanctuary. Once people saw what was there, they wanted to protect it.

Q. Are travel journalists doing a good job of promoting responsible travel?

Tourtellot: I would like to see an increased level of awareness on the part of travel journalists . . . to teach people how to spend their money in a manner that will help maintain the distinctiveness of a place. A question that we're often asked as travel writers is "Aren't you afraid that if you write about a place, you're going to destroy it by sending a lot of people there?" The unfortunate answer is if you don't write about it, somebody else will. There are very few secret places anymore. So we must now understand what the vulnerabilities of a place are before we visit, and to help protect that place as best we can while we're there.

---

[8] A **pebble** is a small round stone.
[9] A **franchise** that sells food has been allowed by another company to sell that company's food.
[10] A **cannery** is factory where food is canned.

LESSON A — UNDERSTANDING THE READING

A | Identifying Main Ideas. Write the correct paragraph letter next to each main idea from the reading (1–7).

| A | B | C | E | F | H | J |

- _C_ 1. Traditional tourism can be harmful to local people and the environment.
- _H_ 2. Well-managed tourism helps to preserve what is special about a place.
- _E_ 3. Geotourism, ecotourism, and sustainable tourism are three different things.
- _J_ 4. Travel writers should promote destinations in ways that will protect them.
- _F_ 5. Badly managed tourism can ruin a place.
- _B_ 6. Tourtellot believes we need a strategy (plan) for dealing with the increase in tourism.
- _A_ 7. An increase in tourism is threatening (harm) some travel destinations.

B | Identifying Supporting Details. Match a paragraph letter from exercise **A** with each supporting detail below (1–6).

- 7 _A_ 1. In 2010, there were over one billion international tourist trips.
- 3 _E_ 2. Geotourism is tourism that sustains or improves a travel destination.
- 4 _J_ 3. Tourists should know if a place is vulnerable before they visit it.
- 2 _H_ 4. Eating at a local restaurant can help to preserve an area's unique character.
- 1 _C_ 5. Large tourist hotels are often owned by companies outside the tourist area.
- 5 _F_ 6. Coastlines can be easily damaged by tourism if it is not well planned.

> **CT Focus**
>
> Writers often contrast the advantages of an idea that they are arguing for with the disadvantages of an alternative. **Showing the drawbacks of an alternative idea** can strengthen a writer's argument.

C | Critical Thinking: Analyzing an Argument. Look at the list of advantages and disadvantages provided in the reading and write each letter (a–f) in the correct place on the lines below.

a. enhances local areas by creating tourist attractions that focus on or preserve the environment and/or historic buildings
b. people spend money that doesn't go to local communities
c. people support the local economy by buying locally made products, eating in local restaurants, and staying in local hotels
d. people don't learn about the local culture
e. development (such as large hotels) can ruin natural areas and threaten marine life and wildlife
f. people meet local residents and learn about the cultures of the places they visit

Advantages of Geotourism: _a, c, f_

Disadvantages of Traditional Tourism: _b, d, e_

D | Critical Thinking: Evaluating an Argument. Discuss these questions in a small group.

1. Do you agree with Tourtellot's arguments regarding geotourism vs. traditional tourism? Can you think of any possible disadvantages of geotourism? Might traditional tourism have any advantages?
2. Which tourist places where you live are well managed or badly managed? Why do you think so?

DEVELOPING READING SKILLS

> **Reading Skill:** Analyzing Causes and Effects
>
> Recognizing causes and effects in a reading passage helps you to understand it better. Writers often use certain words and phrases to signal causes and effects. Look at these sentences from the reading passage.
>
> *Large package tour companies may not always hire local experts and guides.*
> **cause**
>
> **As a result**, *much of the money made from this type of tourism does not stay in the local community.*
> **effect**
>
> The signal phrase *as a result* shows the relationship between the cause and the effect; in this case, it introduces the effect.
>
> These signal words and phrases introduce causes: *if, because, when, as,* and *one effect of.*
>
> These signal words and phrases introduce effects: *as a result, so, therefore, consequently, thus, (this) leads/led to,* and *that is why.*

A | Analyzing. Read the paragraph about ecotourism. Underline words that signal causes and/or effects. Then fill in the causes and effects in the chart.

Because ecotourism can bring significant economic benefits, many local and national governments are looking at ways to preserve their distinctive natural areas. In Costa Rica, for example, the rise of ecotourism led to the creation of several national parks and reserves where wildlife is protected. Ecotourism can also improve the economy at a local level. For example, local people often respond to the growing number of tourists by finding jobs as tour guides or starting small tourist-oriented businesses. Thus, they can increase their income and improve their standard of living.

Cause | **Effect**

ecotourism brings economic benefits

B | Applying. Reread the following paragraphs on page 98 and fill in the effects in the chart.

Cause | **Effect**

F   badly managed tourism

H   well-managed tourism

VIEWING

Galápagos Tourism

▲ Tourists approach a land iguana on North Seymour Island, Galápagos Islands National Park.

Before Viewing

A | Using a Dictionary. The words and expressions in **bold** are used in the video. Match each word or expression with the correct definition. Use your dictionary to help you.

The Galápagos Islands are famous for the unique native plants and animals that live there. Increased tourism brought **revenue** to the islands, but in addition to income, it also brought problems. For example, **contaminants** from gasoline and other fuels caused pollution and killed animals. But an oil spill was **a wake-up call**. Now locals and environmental organizations such as the World Wildlife Fund are making the islands "green," as they work together to **minimize** the impact of tourism on the environment.

1. _____: (noun) an event that changes the way people think about something
2. _____: (noun) money that a company or a government receives from people
3. _____: (verb) reduce something, or prevent it from increasing
4. _____: (noun) substances that cause harm

B | Thinking Ahead. What effect might tourists and tourism activities have on animal species that live on remote islands in the Pacific Ocean? Discuss with a partner.

While Viewing

Read questions 1–4. Think about the answers as you view the video.

1. Why are the animals on the Galápagos Islands special?
2. Why did workers from Ecuador come to the Galápagos Islands?
3. What happened when an oil tanker crashed in the Galápagos Islands?
4. What are people doing to make the Galápagos more "green"?

After Viewing

A | Discuss your answers to questions 1-4 above with a partner.

B | Critical Thinking: Synthesizing. Look back at the reading on pages 97–99. What ideas might Jonathan Tourtellot have to encourage geotourism on the Galápagos Islands?

PREPARING TO READ

LESSON B

A | Building Vocabulary. Find the words in **blue** in the reading passage on pages 104–106. Use the content to guess their meanings. Then write each word below next to its definition (1–10).

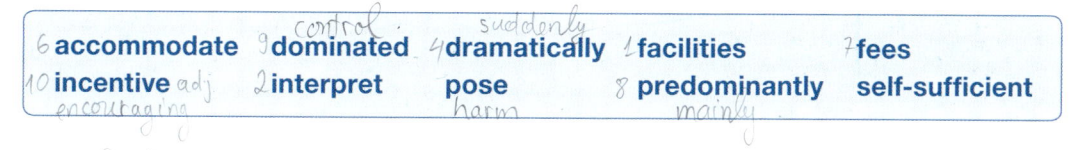

> 6 accommodate   9 dominated *control*   4 dramatically *suddenly*   1 facilities   7 fees
> 10 incentive *adj encouraging*   2 interpret   pose *harm*   8 predominantly *mainly*   self-sufficient

1. _facilities_: (noun) buildings, equipment, or services that are provided for a particular purpose

2. _interpret_: (verb) explain the meaning or significance of something; also, translate something into another language

3. _self-sufficient_: (adjective) able to produce or make everything that is needed

4. _dramatically_: (adverb) done in a sudden and very noticeable way

5. _pose_: (verb) be the cause of something, such as a problem or danger

6. _accommodate_: (verb) provide room or space for people or things

7. _fees_: (noun) money that a person or an organization is paid for a particular job or service

8. _predominantly_: (adverb) mostly; mainly

9. _dominated_: (adjective) controlled (by)

10. _incentive_: (noun) something that encourages you to do something

B | Using Vocabulary. Discuss these questions with a partner.

1. How many different kinds of **accommodation** have you stayed in while traveling?
2. Can you think of any jobs that are **predominantly** male-**dominated**?
3. Does tourism **pose** any problems for communities in your country? Explain your answer.

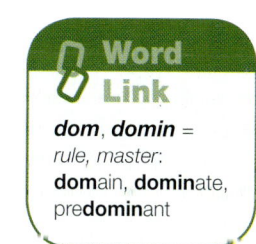

> **Word Link**
> **dom, domin** = rule, master:
> **dom**ain, **domin**ate, pre**domin**ant

C | Brainstorming. Imagine that you are going to create a resort or a hotel in a place that has natural beauty such as a rainforest, a beach, or a mountainside. Discuss answers with a partner. What kinds of issues will you consider? How will you protect the environment? What services will you provide for your guests?

D | Predicting. Read the title and the three headings in the reading passage on pages 104–106 and answer the questions. As you read, check your predictions.

1. What three places does the reading passage discuss?
2. What do you think the three places have in common?

LESSON B READING

Geotourism in Action: Three Success Stories

Tribal leader Moi Enomenga brings together conservation and ecotourism at an award-winning Ecolodge.

As the negative effects of tourism become increasingly acknowledged, more effort is being made to create tourist experiences that enhance—rather than harm—local cultures and environments. The following examples—from three different continents—demonstrate how innovative local programs can promote sustainable tourism.

1 ECUADOR
Huaorani Ecolodge

Moi Vicente Enomenga was born near Coca in the Ecuadorian Amazon. At just 18, he became a leader among the Huaorani—one of the most isolated native communities on Earth—and quickly recognized the dangers presented to the local culture, particularly through the encroachment of the oil industry. Enomenga soon came to believe that ecotourism could play a significant role in helping to preserve his local culture. In 2010, he and his partners built the Huaorani Ecolodge. Their goal—to provide income and an incentive for the local community to protect the environment through sustainable tourism.

Owned and operated by local Huaorani people, the small ecolodge has five traditionally built, palm-thatched[1] cabins, which can accommodate up to ten visitors. Solar panels supply electricity, and the lodge provides environmentally friendly soaps and shampoos. Visitors can buy locally made handicrafts, such as woven bags and necklaces, from the community market, thus providing employment to Huaorani families. Local guides teach tourists rainforest survival skills, including how to set animal traps, make fire without matches, and build a shelter in minutes. Guides also identify and explain the uses of medicinal plants.

Visitors to the Huaorani Ecolodge can also take a "toxic tour"—a canoe trip that shows some ways that the oil industry has dramatically impacted Huaorani

---
[1] If a building is **palm-thatched**, it has a roof made from the leaves of a palm tree.

104 | UNIT 5

▲ The three founders of 3 Sisters Adventure Trekking: Lucky, Nicky, and Dicky Chhetri

lands, including deforestation and building roads through former Huaorani land. This trip shows visitors the continuing threat posed by outside companies and developers, and reminds them why sustainable tourism is so important.

2 NEPAL

3 Sisters Adventure Trekking

Nepal has been an important tourist destination for trekking[2] and mountaineering for over a hundred years. Until recently, however, the tour guides and porters[3] were predominantly male. In 1993, three sisters—Lucky, Dicky, and Nicky Chhetri—were running a restaurant and travel lodge in Pokhara, Nepal. When some female trekkers staying at their lodge complained of poor treatment by male porters, the sisters got the idea to start their own trekking business—one run by women, for women. They launched their business venture—3 Sisters Adventure Trekking—with two main goals: to give local women opportunities to work in the male-dominated tourism industry, and to give female trekkers the choice of female guides for greater comfort and security.

The trekking company was Nepal's first all-female trekking business. The sisters also established a non-profit organization—Empowering Women of Nepal (EWN)—to train and hire local women as trekking guides. The training program includes classes in English conversation, leadership, health, and nutrition. It also emphasizes ecological awareness and conservation by teaching participants about water sanitation, waste management, and alternative fuel sources. To discourage the use of plastic bottles, for example, trainees are taught to use iodine[4] to purify water, thus reducing litter on the mountains.

At the end of the program, the trainees enter an apprenticeship with 3 Sisters Adventure Trekking, where they get on-the-job experience as guides and earn wages equal to those of their male counterparts. Lucky Chhetri sums up the program's purpose: "Our aim has been, and continues to be, to empower and develop women through tourism and to encourage sustainable tourism in remote areas." Through their

[2] **Trekking** is traveling on foot across difficult countryside, such as mountains.

[3] **Porters** are people who carry things, such as luggage.

[4] **Iodine** is a dark-colored substance used in medicine. It purifies water to make it drinkable.

THE BUSINESS OF TOURISM | 105

LESSON B   READING

apprenticeship, the trainees gain immediate economic benefits, but they also develop the skills they need to become independent entrepreneurs. Some program graduates use their earnings to continue their education, while others start their own businesses.

3 Sisters Adventure Trekking offers its guides insurance, tuition fees for their children, and a savings program. Improving employees' social and economic situations—empowering them to be independent, confident, and self-sufficient—also benefits their families and community. Furthermore, the interaction between local guides and tourists from all over the world creates a vital cultural exchange. "I learned to become an ambassador for my country," says one of the graduates of the 3 Sisters program.

3 AUSTRALIA
Anangu Tours

At the base of Uluru, a great stone monolith[5] 1,142 feet (348 meters) high and 6 miles (9.7 kilometers) around, Anangu guide Sammy Wilson addresses a group of tourists in English. "I'm on my land, so I'm going to be speaking in my language." Wilson continues the tour in his native *Yankunytjatjara* language while his interpreter translates.

Most people know Uluru as Ayer's Rock, the icon[6] of Australia's Red Center region. But for the Anangu—meaning "we people"—Uluru is the heart of a region where they have lived for over 20,000 years. Anangu Tours—owned and operated by local Aboriginal people—provides tourists to Uluru with an authentic cultural learning experience. The tours are not in English because for the Anangu people, language is an essential matter of cultural pride.

As Wilson leads the tour group to the base of the huge rock, he explains the traditional body of Aboriginal "creation law" called *Tjukurpa*, which includes economic, ecological, and religious rules for living. Tjukurpa tells the story of how the world was created and defines relationships between people and land. Where outsiders look at Uluru and see rock, the Anangu see expressions of Tjukurpa—spear marks, footprints, and ancestral beings turned to stone.

▲ At Uluru National Park, an Aboriginal guide explains the significance of the monument to groups of tourists.

Unlike other tour companies and tourists, Anangu guides do not let visitors climb the rock, as it is against Tjukurpa. Instead, Anangu guides lead tourists around Uluru on paths their ancestors walked. The guides interpret cave paintings and explain natural foods and medicines—for example, how to make bread from a local grass seed and how to treat sore muscles and colds with a native *irramunga* plant. Anangu guides also teach bush[7] skills, such as how to throw a spear and make a fire.

In sharing the area's heritage, Anangu Tours gives tourists a way to experience Aboriginal culture while respecting local traditions. The company contributes profits to local recreation and education facilities and has helped establish the first Aboriginal secondary school in the area. In 2004, Anangu Tours' efforts were recognized when it won the 2004 World Legacy Award for Heritage Tourism. Says Jonathan Tourtellot, a co-creator of the World Legacy Awards, "We want to reward the people who are doing trailblazing work in forging[8] mutually beneficial relationships between tourism and the destinations on which tourism depends."

[5] A **monolith** is a very large, upright piece of stone.
[6] If something is an **icon**, it is important as a symbol of a particular thing or place.
[7] In Australia, the **bush** refers to the wild, uncultivated parts of the county.
[8] If a person or an institution **forges** an agreement with another, they create the agreement usually after a lot of hard work.

UNDERSTANDING THE READING

A | Identifying Main Ideas. How are the three organizations examples of successful geotourism? Match the sentence parts.

1. Huaorani Ecolodge __c__
2. 3 Sisters Adventure Trekking __a__
3. Anangu Tours __b__

a. empowers women and teaches them about conservation. *(give power)*

b. teaches visitors about local culture and to respect local traditions.

c. preserves the rain forest and provides employment for local people.

B | Identifying Meaning from Context. Find and underline the following words in the reading passage on pages 104–106. Use context to help you identify the part of speech and meaning of each word. Write your answers, and then check your answers in a dictionary.

1. encroachment (paragraph B)   Part of speech: _____
   Meaning: _harming_

2. lodge (paragraph C)   Part of speech: _____
   Meaning: _small house, accommodation_

3. handicrafts (paragraph C)   Part of speech: _____
   Meaning: _handmade products_

4. trekkers (paragraph E)   Part of speech: _____
   Meaning: _travellers who travel on foot, climbers_

5. launched (paragraph E)   Part of speech: _____
   Meaning: _started, began_

6. apprenticeship (paragraph G)   Part of speech: _____
   Meaning: _training program (co-op)_

7. entrepreneurs (paragraph G)   Part of speech: _____
   Meaning: _people who open their own business_

8. ambassador (paragraph H)   Part of speech: _____
   guía
   Meaning: _representative_

LESSON B UNDERSTANDING THE READING

C | Identifying Supporting Details. Find details in the reading passage to answer the following questions.

1. How do local Huaorani people benefit from the lodge?
   get job, get money

2. What kinds of things can visitors to the Huaorani Ecolodge do?
   buy local handicrafts, learn about rainforest survival skill, take "toxic tour"

3. What is threatening Huaorani lands?
   oil industry (deforestation - building roads)

4. What does the sisters' non-profit organization EWN teach local women?
   English conversation, leadership, health, nutrition

5. What are some of the things that EWN trainees do when they finish their apprenticeship?
   continue or start their own business.

6. What do some other tour companies do when they go to Ayer's Rock that Anangu Tours does *not* do?
   climb the rock

7. How does Anangu Tours benefit the local community?
   Company contributes profit to local recreation & education facilities & help establish the 1st Aboriginal secondary school in area

D | Identifying Causes and Effects. Use information from the reading to complete the effects in the chart.

Cause	Effect(s)
female trekkers complained of poor treatment by male porters	
3 Sisters Adventure Trekking started EWN	

E | Critical Thinking: Making Inferences. Discuss the questions with a partner.

1. What message is Anangu Tours giving to tourists by conducting tours in the local language?
2. Why might the Anangu people believe climbing Uluru is against Tjukurpa?

F | Critical Thinking: Synthesizing. Discuss how each program in "Geotourism in Action" follows Jonathan Tourtellot's definition of geotourism on page 98.

G | Discussing Ideas. Are there things tourists do in your country that local people find disrespectful? Why? Discuss in a small group.

EXPLORING WRITTEN ENGLISH

LESSON C

> **GOAL: Writing a Short Cause-Effect Essay**
> In this lesson, you are going to plan, write, revise, and edit a short essay on the following topic:
> **What are the possible effects of geotourism for (a specific area in) your country?**

A | **Brainstorming.** Think of two places in your country that could benefit from geotourism. List the possible effects of geotourism in each place.

_____

_____

> **Free Writing.** Describe a place from your brainstorming notes. What is surprising or interesting about it? Write for five minutes.

B | Read the information in the box. Then decide which sentence in each pair below (1–4) is a cause and which is an effect. Then combine the sentences using *if* clauses.

> **Language for Writing:** Using *If . . . , (then) . . .*
>
> One way to express a cause-effect relationship that is generally true is to use sentences with *if*. In these sentences, the *if* clause introduces a condition or cause that leads to the effect or result expressed in the other clause.
>
>   ***If*** *tourism is managed well, both tourists and local people benefit.*
>   **cause**   **effect**
>
>   ***If*** *you spend your money at local restaurants, (**then**) your money stays in the community.*
>   **cause**   **effect**
>
> You can also reverse the order of the clauses (without *then*):
>
>   *Both tourists and local people benefit **if** tourism is managed well.*
>   **effect**   **cause**
>
> You can also use a modal (*can, should, might, must*) in the effect clause.
>
>   ***If*** *tourism is badly managed, it **can** destroy a place.*
>   **cause**   **effect**
>
> Remember: Use a comma when the *if* clause comes first. Use the present tense in the *if* clause and the present tense or a modal in the effect clause.

1. You buy local handicrafts. You support the local economy.
2. Forests and beaches can be ruined. Too many people visit them.
3. More women can enjoy trekking. The porters are female.
4. Tourists can learn about local customs. They stay at Huaorani Ecolodge.

C | Rewrite three sentences from your free writing using *if* clauses.

THE BUSINESS OF TOURISM | 109

LESSON C — EXPLORING WRITTEN ENGLISH

Writing Skill: Writing Well-Developed Body Paragraphs

As you learned in previous units, the main idea of each body paragraph in an essay reflects and supports the thesis statement. A **well-developed body paragraph** includes supporting ideas that give information and details about the main idea. Body paragraph sentences include details, examples, and facts that give the reader a clear understanding of the main idea. They also answer questions that the reader might have.

One strategy for making sure that you have a well-developed body paragraph is to think of possible questions a reader might have about each sentence in your paragraph. If your sentences do not adequately answer all possible questions, then you need to add more details, facts, or examples.

D | Critical Thinking: Analyzing. Read the paragraph below about an ecotourism success story. Some information is missing from this paragraph. Match the writer's research notes with a reader's questions about the paragraph. Then rewrite the paragraph, adding the information from the notes.

_____ How did the community benefit?

__c__ How much has disappeared?

Kakum National Park, located in the Upper Guinean Rainforest of West Africa, offers one example of the direct benefits of ecotourism. According to the organization Conservation International (CI), much of this rainforest has disappeared. CI partnered to raise money to make the park more attractive to tourists. The community benefited as a result of the project. Afterwards, there were many more visitors to the park.

_____ How many more visitors were there?

_____ Who did they partner with?

_____ How did they make the park more attractive to tourists?

Research notes on Kakum National Park

a. fewer than 1000 visitors in 1991; 90,000 in 2000
b. local people did the work; the project used local materials
c. more than 80 percent of rainforest has disappeared; cause: deforestation
d. 1990s: CI partnered with various national and international organizations; got money
e. built visitor's center, wildlife exhibitions, restaurants, shops, camping facilities, a special walkway (takes visitors through treetops of rainforest)

WRITING TASK: Drafting

LESSON C

A | **Planning.** Follow the steps to make notes for your short essay.

Step 1 In the outline below, note the place you are going to write about, and note two possible effects of geotourism from your brainstorming notes on page 109.

Step 2 Complete the thesis statement in the outline.

Step 3 Write topic sentences for each of your body paragraphs.

Step 4 Now write two examples or details that explain the possible effects.

Place: _____

Two most important effects of geotourism

1: _____

2: _____

Thesis statement: The possible effects of geotourism in _____ include _____ and _____.

Body Paragraph 1: Topic sentence: One possible effect of geotourism in _____ is _____.

Detail 1: _____

Detail 2: _____

Body Paragraph 2: Topic sentence: Another possible effect of geotourism in _____ is _____.

Detail 1: _____

Detail 2: _____

Step 5 Look at your free writing. Use this information to begin your introductory paragraph. Make one or more surprising statements about the place you have chosen.

B | **Draft 1.** Use the outline above to write a first draft.

LESSON C

WRITING TASK: Revising

C | Critical Thinking: Analyzing. Work with a partner. Read the student's essay about the effects of increased tourism in an area of California. Then follow the steps to analyze the paragraphs.

The northwestern coast of California is a very attractive travel destination. Increasing numbers of tourists are visiting this area to hike in the redwood forests and along the white sand beaches. As a result, people who live in this area are very concerned about the effects of mass tourism. Local residents are worried that the increased tourism will weaken the local economy and damage the natural beauty of the beaches and the forests.

If tourists stay at big chain hotels instead of smaller local hotels, and eat only at chain restaurants, then the money they spend for food and lodging goes to businesses that are probably not locally owned. If smaller locally owned businesses aren't successful, they are less able to hire local employees. Consequently, local businesses do not benefit from the increased tourism. In this way, traditional mass tourism can weaken the local economy.

Another effect of increased tourism in the northwestern coast is the destruction of the natural beauty of the beaches and the forest. If too many people visit an area, they can ruin it. They leave garbage everywhere. Garbage makes an area look unattractive, and it also harms the local wildlife. In addition, if companies build chain hotels and restaurants on the beach or in the forest, they will have to remove trees, rocks, and other natural features. If mass tourism is not managed well, it will destroy the local economy, ruin the natural beauty of the area, cause pollution, and harm wildlife.

Step 1 Underline the thesis statement.

Step 2 Circle the two reasons in the thesis statement that support the writer's position or opinion on the topic.

Step 3 Underline the topic sentences in the two body paragraphs.

Step 4 Circle the key words in each topic sentence that match the key words in the thesis statement.

Step 5 In the first body paragraph, check (✔) sentences that answer possible reader questions about the main idea of the paragraph. Then do the same for the second paragraph.

Step 6 Does the writer provide enough support for their position? Are there any other questions a reader might have?

D | Revising. Follow steps 1–6 in exercise **C** to analyze your own paragraphs.

E | Peer Evaluation. Exchange your first draft with a partner and follow the steps below.

Step 1 Read your partner's paragraphs and tell him or her one thing that you liked about it.

Step 2 Complete the outline showing the ideas that your partner's paragraphs describe.

Place: _____

Two most important effects of geotourism

1: _____
_____

2: _____
_____

Thesis statement: The possible effects of geotourism in _____ include _____ and _____.

Body Paragraph 1: Topic sentence: One possible effect of geotourism in _____ is _____.

Detail 1: _____
_____

Detail 2: _____
_____

Body Paragraph 2: Topic sentence: Another possible effect of geotourism in _____ is _____.

Detail 1: _____
_____

Detail 2: _____
_____

Step 3 Compare this outline with the one that your partner created in exercise **A** on page 111.

Step 4 The two outlines should be similar. If they aren't, discuss how they differ.

LESSON C — WRITING TASK: Editing

F | Draft 2. Write a second draft of your paragraphs. Use what you learned from the peer evaluation activity and your answers to exercise **D**. Make any other necessary changes.

G | Editing Practice. Read the information in the box. Then find and correct one mistake with *if* clauses in each of the sentences (1–5).

> In sentences with *if* clauses that describe general truths, remember:
> - that the *if* clause introduces the condition or cause.
> - to use a comma when the *if* clause comes first.
> - to use the present tense in both clauses, or the present tense in the *if* clause and a modal in the result clause.

1. Prices are too high, if people might stop traveling.
2. If travel journalists write about the importance of protecting destinations they educate tourists.
3. If tourists only ate at chain restaurants, they don't learn anything about the local food.
4. Tourists are disrespectful of the local culture, if they climb Ayer's Rock.
5. Local communities can benefit if tourism promoted local industries.

H | Editing Checklist. Use the checklist to find errors in your second draft.

Editing Checklist	Yes	No
1. Are all the words spelled correctly?		
2. Is the first word of every sentence capitalized?		
3. Does every sentence end with the correct punctuation?		
4. Do your subjects and verbs agree?		
5. Did you use *if* clauses correctly?		
6. Are verb tenses correct?		

I | Final Draft. Now use your Editing Checklist to write a third draft of your paragraphs. Make any other necessary changes.

Video Scripts

UNIT 1
Elephant Orphans

Narrator: It's daybreak at The David Sheldrick Wildlife Trust on the edge of Nairobi's National Park. Orphaned elephants and their human caretakers wake up to a beautiful African morning.

Little Shimba came here last September when he was only six weeks old. He was found near his dead mother in the Tsavo National Park. Ten-month-old Chuyla was found stuck in a water hole. She had been orphaned days earlier when her mother was killed by poachers. Many of the orphans here had mothers killed by poachers.

In all, more than 100 orphaned elephants have been saved by The David Sheldrick Wildlife Trust. Eighty of these elephants have survived. And it's not as easy as it seems. Elephant babies stay with their mothers for years. The fat content in the milk of nursing mother elephants varies depending on the baby's age.

Daphne Sheldrick founded The David Sheldrick Wildlife Trust in 1977, in memory of her husband. It took her more than two decades to find the right milk formula—and care—needed to keep orphaned elephants alive.

Daphne Sheldrick: I discovered how to raise an infant African elephant just through trial and error. We found that giving them cow's milk killed them straight away. And then baby milk started coming on to the market for cows' milk sensitive human children.

Narrator: An infant elephant consumes 24 pints of specially formulated milk every 24 hours. When the elephant is six months old, it consumes even more milk. At this point, dried coconut and cooked oatmeal porridge are added to the milk formula. Besides large amounts of food, growing elephants also need a lot of interaction with caregivers. Elephants are social creatures, so the keepers are by their sides 24 hours a day—just as a mother elephant would stay close to her own children.

A blanket mimics maternal warmth when caregivers feed the elephants. The babies hang their trunks on it just as they would lay them across their own mother's belly. And like human children, young elephants like to play. Some experts believe that elephants have a complex social and emotional life similar to humans.

Edwin Lusichi: The care we're giving them is the same as we give to human babies. We feed them, we nurse them, we sleep with them in the same house. We lie down sometimes on the mattresses. We cover them with the blankets just like we do to our human babies. And they behave like human babies: What you tell them not to do is what they want to do. Where you want them not to go is where they want to go.

Narrator: Edwin Lusichi has been at The Trust since 1999. There are 51 keepers here in all. Their task is to care for the elephants until they leave and join other elephants in the wild. The reintroduction back to the wild can take up to 10 years. Some elephants have gone on to successfully reproduce.

Thirty years ago, it's estimated that about three million elephants roamed through Africa. Today, there are only about 250,000 left. The great beasts were slaughtered for their ivory tusks, and for meat. Much of their habitat has been destroyed by human development. These dangers continue to this day.

After a long day, the orphans are ready for some much needed rest. The littlest elephants go to bed with a caring member of their adoptive family. Like human babies, they will wake periodically during the night in search of comfort and food. Adolescents sleep together.

Shimba takes a little snack before bedtime. These orphans are all safe here--for the time being. The Trust hopes these young animals will have a bright future, under the African sky.

UNIT 2
Columbus DNA

Narrator: There's more to bones than meets the eye. At the forensic medical lab of Granada University, scientists clean away centuries of contamination. Underneath lies the DNA that could prove where Christopher Columbus is buried and where he was born.

Dr. Jose Antonio Lorente: There is no doubt that this is an exciting moment for science and for the scientists to be here and to try and solve this long-lasting mystery.

Narrator: The Spanish monarchy financed the voyage that led Columbus to the Americas. At Palos de la Frontera, life-size replicas of the Pinta, Niña, and Santa Maria are moored. The tiny fleet of small ships is a reminder that crossing the Atlantic in 1492 was a remarkable achievement.

The Spanish revere Columbus as one of their own.

Marshall Castro (translated): He opened up an entire world. It is understandable that there is an immense continent somehow spiritually tied to this figure. That's why it's hardly surprising that practically all important cities of Spain, the U.S., and Latin America have erected monuments in his name.

Video Scripts

Narrator: The Cathedral of Seville contains what Spain claims are the remains of Christopher Columbus. At the Cathedral's door of St. Christopher it reads that Columbus is here. But this elaborate tomb apparently isn't what the great explorer had in mind.

Columbus wanted to be buried on Hispaniola, the island he had named for Spain, which today includes Haiti and the Dominican Republic. Columbus was originally buried in Spain, but was later buried in Hispaniola according to his wishes.

In 1795 Spain ceded the island to France and brought his remains back to Europe. But the Dominican Republic claims the Spanish rescued the wrong bones from inside the Cathedral of Santa Maria, and that the real Columbus now lies inside a mausoleum that bears his name.

In Spain, Dr. Lorente prepares to unravel the mystery by analyzing the recently unearthed DNA of Columbus's known relatives.

Dr. Lorente: Genetically it's very easy. The problem is when you have to deal with bones. These bones are 500 years old ones. They are very degraded, they are contaminated, and when we turn these into dust, it's very hard to work with them.

Narrator: Getting permission to compare his findings with the presumed bones of Columbus in the Dominican Republic has proven difficult. Authorities there have resisted the transfer of bones due to the risk of contamination or deterioration, and there are no grounds to expect a conclusive outcome.

Marshall Castro (translated): The controversy over where Columbus is from is even more important than where he's buried. It is the enigma that most troubles historians.

Narrator: At the Monastery of La Rábida, where Columbus lived before sailing to America, monks take questions in stride. They find peace in their faith that the national hero depicted here in modern murals now rests in a higher place. Even so, you can't help but wonder what the explorer would make of the competing claims to his name and his remains.

UNIT 3 Solar Solutions

Narrator: This is the Egypt familiar to most people. Cairo is a big, busy city. But there's a whole other world up here, high on the city's rooftops.

Many Egyptians use the space on rooftops for water tanks, satellite dishes, and even livestock. The garbage piled everywhere is considered valuable because it's often recycled and reused. Cairo has been "going green" long before it became fashionable.

That's why National Geographic Emerging Explorer Thomas Taha Culhane's program has been so special. He's been helping lower-income Egyptians build solar-powered water heaters—partly out of recycled trash—and putting them on their rooftops.

Thomas Taha Culhane: People will come to this community, and they'll look on the rooftops and they'll say why is there so much trash on the roofs, but if you talk to the homeowners they'll say, "What trash? I'm saving for the future when I can figure out a good way to use it." So there is no trash. And that is, I think, the message that inner-city Cairo, and the informal communities of Cairo, have for the world. Forget this idea that there is garbage. One man's garbage is another's gold mine.

Narrator: The water heaters take advantage of Egypt's great national resource—abundant sunshine. When the system is placed just right . . .

Culhane: Oh, you're good. You are good. You know what you're at? 39.9 degrees. Whoa. Whoa.

Narrator: Solar panels heat up water that circulates through metal tubes, eventually filling a tank with extremely hot water.

Culhane: This is a hand-made solar hot water system, and it's made out of local community materials, recycled materials, and even some garbage. And we put it together as cheaply as possible to demonstrate that anybody can make a solar hot water system; that renewable energy is not some exotic technology; that it can be made from found materials and it works.

Narrator: The solar heaters allow urban dwellers access to a plentiful supply of hot water. The heaters improve the quality of life and sanitation, and they cut down on potential energy costs. Culhane says the only problem is the dust from the nearby desert that coats the city and the panels.

Culhane: Solar works tremendously well if there's sun. Cairo has sun. But it also has dust. Until people appreciate that, they won't come up and just do the simple thing of just wiping the dust away. So really it's just a matter of a few seconds to wipe it down and then the system is functioning again. But because people don't do this, they will say, "Solar does not work in Cairo." And what we have to do is get them to be as aware of the need to just dust these as they are dusting their kitchen table. Once they accept that, solar is a no-brainer here. It's an easy thing to do.

Narrator: Culhane hopes the water heater project will lead to other innovations using recycled materials. As the saying goes, one man's garbage is another man's treasure.

UNIT 4: Hurricanes

Narrator: Violent winds, driving rain, killer waves. These are the hallmarks of a hurricane. Also called cyclones or typhoons, hurricanes are giant storms that form in the world's tropical seas. An average hurricane releases as much energy in a day as the explosion of half a million small atomic bombs.

Hurricanes form in the summer and fall, when the sun heats vast stretches of tropical ocean to over 82 degrees. Warm, moist air rises over these hot spots, creating thunderstorms. Upper level winds and surface winds then come together, forming a circular pattern of clouds known as a tropical depression. When the winds exceed 39 miles per hour, a tropical storm has developed. When the winds reach 74 miles per hour, a hurricane is officially born.

Inside the storm, bands of rain up to 300 miles long meet in the eye wall, the most violent section. Here, winds of up to 200 miles per hour spiral upward. Within the center of the hurricane, dry air blowing downward creates a strangely calm area called the eye. Fully formed, a hurricane may stretch over 500 miles in diameter—a storm nearly the size of Texas—and reach a height of 9 miles.

Most of these storms spin out over the open sea. But in an average year, two or three will strike the mainland of North America. When they do, the damage can be catastrophic. Most dangerous is the storm surge, a wall of water that sweeps across the coastline where a hurricane makes landfall.

About 45,000 people were killed by hurricanes in the 20th century, including some 15,000 in the United States. Hurricanes are also costly in dollars. 1992's Hurricane Andrew was the most expensive natural disaster in U.S. history, causing more than 25 billion dollars' worth of damage.

Scientists are searching for better ways to predict the path of a hurricane. Special planes called "hurricane hunters" fly directly into these monster storms and drop sensors to measure wind speed, temperature and air pressure—providing vital clues to the hurricane's direction.

New 3-D models are also helping scientists understand this awesome force of nature, and provide quicker and more accurate warnings to anyone unlucky enough to be caught in its path.

UNIT 5: Galápagos Tourism

Narrator: The Galápagos is a collection of 13 main islands in the Pacific Ocean. They are a thousand kilometers—or six hundred miles—from the coast of Ecuador in South America.

The Galápagos is famous for the animal species that live here. Because the islands are isolated, animals evolved into unique species that do not exist anywhere else in the world.

Narrator: But another species is invading these tropical islands . . . humans. They've been living here for more than a century. But in the past few decades, tourism has increased dramatically. And workers from Ecuador have come, too, to open businesses and provide services for the tourists. Some estimate the local population on the islands has increased by as much as 300 percent.

Lauren Spurrier: In the 1980s, there was a local population of about 3,000 people living here on the islands, and today, we have a local population of more than 25,000 people.

Narrator: Tourism brings much-needed revenue. But all these people generate pollution through vehicle emissions and energy consumption. And like almost all humans, they create trash. Environmentalists worry that tourism is having a negative impact on the islands' original inhabitants—the animals.

Recently an oil tanker that was trying to deliver fuel to the Galápagos crashed. The oil spill that resulted from the crash eventually killed an estimated 60 percent of nearby iguanas. Researchers now say even a small amount of pollution can harm the islands' famous animal species.

Fortunately, the oil spill turned out to be a wake-up call. Now, with a series of ambitious projects, environmentalists and corporations are working together with the Ecuadorian government to minimize human impact. The goal is to end the use of fossil fuels on the Galápagos in the next decade and to use only renewable, non-polluting energy.

The goal is to make the islands "green." For example, these modern oil tanks replace rusty older ones that were about to fall into the sea. Contaminants in the fuel are removed to reduce pollution. An ultra-modern gas station has barriers to contain leaks. There's an ambitious plan to convert boat engines to cleaner and more efficient engines. And to replace cars on the islands with low-emissions vehicles.

Video Scripts

A World Wildlife Fund recycling campaign is teaching islanders about the importance of preserving the natural beauty of their islands. For example, Lourdes Peñaherrera and her family have won a World Wildlife Fund award for reducing the amount of waste they produce.

Lourdes Peñaherrera (translated): "Not only us, but the whole community has to recycle," she says. "It's to protect the environment. Almost everybody in our neighborhood does it now."

Narrator: Environmentalists say humans will continue to have an impact on the Galápagos, but local cooperation combined with the help of international environmental organizations such as the World Wildlife Fund may help to control the impact.

There once were no people on these isolated islands, but now the world has arrived. Instead of ruining the Galápagos Islands, perhaps with a united effort, they will save them.

Independent Student Handbook

Contents

Tips for Reading and Note Taking

Reading fluently	242
Thinking critically	242
Note taking	242
Learning vocabulary	243
Common affixes	243

Tips for Writing and Research

Features of academic writing	244
Proofreading tips	244
Research and referencing	245
Common signal phrases	246

Reading and Writing Reference 247

Independent Student Handbook

Tips for Reading and Note Taking

Reading fluently

Why develop your reading speed?

Reading slowly, one word at a time, makes it difficult to get an overall sense of the meaning of a text. As a result, reading becomes more challenging and less interesting than if you read at a faster pace. In general, it is a good idea to first skim a text for the gist, and then read it again more closely so that you can focus on the most relevant details.

Strategies for improving reading speed:

- Try to read groups of words rather than individual words.
- Keep your eyes moving forward. Read through to the end of each sentence or paragraph instead of going back to reread words or phrases within the sentence or paragraph.
- Read selectively. Skip functional words (articles, prepositions, etc.) and focus on words and phrases carrying meaning—the content words.
- Use clues in the text—such as highlighted text (**bold** words, words in *italics*, etc.)—to help you know which parts might be important and worth focusing on.
- Use section headings, as well as the first and last lines of paragraphs, to help you understand how the text is organized.
- Use context and other clues such as affixes and part of speech to guess the meaning of unfamiliar words and phrases. Try to avoid using a dictionary if you are reading quickly for overall meaning.

Thinking critically

As you read, ask yourself questions about what the writer is saying, and how and why the writer is presenting the information at hand.

Important critical thinking skills for academic reading and writing:

- Analyzing: Examining a text in close detail in order to identify key points, similarities, and differences.
- Evaluating: Using evidence to decide how relevant, important, or useful something is. This often involves looking at reasons for and against something.
- Inferring: "Reading between the lines;" in other words, identifying what a writer is saying indirectly, or *implicitly*, rather than directly, or *explicitly*.
- Synthesizing: Gathering appropriate information and ideas from more than one source and making a judgment, summary, or conclusion based on the evidence.
- Reflecting: Relating ideas and information in a text to your own personal experience and preconceptions (i.e., the opinions or beliefs you had before reading the text).

Note taking

Taking notes of key points and the connections between them will help you better understand the overall meaning and organization of a text. Note taking also enables you to record the most important ideas and information for future use such as when you are preparing for an exam or completing a writing assignment.

Techniques for effective note taking:

- As you read, underline or highlight important information such as dates, names, places, and other facts.
- Take notes in the margin—as you read, note the main idea and supporting details next to each paragraph. Also note your own ideas or questions about the paragraph.
- On paper or on a computer, paraphrase the key points of the text in your own words.
- Keep your notes brief—include short headings to organize the information, key words and phrases (not full sentences), and abbreviations and symbols. (See next page for examples.)
- Note sources of information precisely. Be sure to include page numbers, names of relevant people and places, and quotations.
- Make connections between key points with techniques such as using arrows and colors to connect ideas and drawing circles or squares around related information.
- Use a graphic organizer to summarize a text, particularly if it follows a pattern such as cause-effect, comparison-contrast, or chronological sequence. (See page 77 for more information.)
- Use your notes to write a summary of the passage in order to remember what you learned.

Independent Student Handbook

Useful abbreviations

approx.	approximately	impt	important
ca.	about, around (date / year)	incl.	including
cd	could	info	information
Ch.	Chapter	p. (pp.)	page (pages)
devt	development	para.	paragraph
e.g./ex.	example	ppl	people
etc.	and others / and the rest	re:	regarding, concerning
excl.	excluding	res	research
govt	government	wd	would
hist	history	yr(s)	years(s)
i.e.	that is; in other words	C20	20th century

Useful symbols

→	leads to / causes
↑	increases / increased
↓	decreases / decreased
& or +	and
∴	therefore
b/c	because
w/	with
=	is the same as
>	is more than
<	is less than
~	is approximately / about

Learning vocabulary

More than likely, you will not remember a new word or phrase after reading or hearing it once. You need to use the word several times before it enters your long-term memory.

Strategies for learning vocabulary:

- Use flash cards. Write the words you want to learn on one side of an index card. Write the definition and/or an example sentence that uses the word on the other side. Use your flash cards to test your knowledge of new vocabulary.
- Keep a vocabulary journal. When you come across a new word or phrase, write a short definition of the word (in English, if possible) and the sentence or situation where you found it (its context). Write another sentence of your own that uses the word. Include any common collocations. (See the Word Partners boxes in this book for examples of collocations.)
- Make word webs (or "word maps").
- Use memory aids. It may be easier to remember a word or phrase if you use a memory aid, or *mnemonic*. For example, if you want to learn the idiom *keep an eye on someone*, which means to "watch someone carefully," you might picture yourself putting your eyeball on someone's shoulder so that you can watch the person carefully. The stranger the picture is, the more you will remember it!

Common affixes

Some words contain an affix at the start of the word (*prefix*) and/or at the end (*suffix*). These affixes can be useful for guessing the meaning of unfamiliar words and for expanding your vocabulary. In general, a prefix affects the meaning of a word, whereas a suffix affects its part of speech. See the Word Link boxes in this book for specific examples.

Prefix	Meaning	Example	Suffix	Part of Speech	Example
com- con-	with	combine	-able	adjective	dependable
commun-	sharing	communicate	-al	adjective	traditional
con-	together, with	construct	-ate	verb	differentiate
dom-/domin-	rule, master	dominate	-ed	adjective	involved
em- / en-	making, putting	empower, endanger	-eer	noun	pioneer, volunteer
ex-	away, from, out	external	-ent / -ant	adjective	confident, significant
extra-	outside of	extracurricular	-er	noun	researcher
in-	not	independent	-ful	adjective	grateful
lingu-	language	bilingual	-ical	adjective	practical
inter-	between	interactive	-ity	noun	reality
minim-	smallest	minimal	-ive	adjective	positive
migr-	moving	immigrant	-ize	verb	socialize
mot-	moving	motion	-ly	adverb	definitely
pre-	before	prevent	-ment	noun	achievement
re-	back, again	restore	-tion	noun	prevention
sci-	knowing	conscience			
sur-	above	surface			
trans-	across	transfer			
un-	not	uninvolved			
vict-/vinc-	conquering	victory			
vid-/vis-	seeing	video, vision			

Independent Student Handbook

Tips for Writing and Research

Features of academic writing

There are many types of academic writing (descriptive, argumentative/persuasive, narrative, etc.), but most types share similar characteristics.

Generally, in academic writing you should:

- write in full sentences.
- use formal English. (Avoid slang or conversational expressions such as *kind of*.)
- be clear and coherent—keep to your main point; avoid technical words that the reader may not know.
- use signal words and phrases to connect your ideas. (See examples on page 246.)
- have a clear point (main idea) for each paragraph.
- be objective—most academic writing uses a neutral, impersonal point of view, so avoid overuse of personal pronouns (*I*, *we*, *you*) and subjective language such as *nice* or *terrible*.
- use facts, examples, and expert opinions to support your argument.
- show where the evidence or opinions come from. (*According to the 2009 World Database Survey,. . . .*)
- show that you have considered other viewpoints.

Generally, in academic writing you should not:

- use abbreviations or language used in texting. (Use *that is* rather than *i.e.*, and *in my opinion*, not *IMO*.)
- use contractions. (Use *is not* rather than *isn't*.)
- be vague. (*A man made the first cell-phone call a few decades ago.* -> *An inventor named Martin Cooper made the first cell-phone call in 1973.*)
- include several pronoun references in a single sentence. (*He thinks it's a better idea than the other one, but I agree with her.*)
- start sentences with *or*, *and*, or *but*.
- apologize to the reader. (*I'm sorry I don't know much about this, but . . .*) In academic writing, it is important to sound confident about what you are saying!

Proofreading tips

Capitalization

Remember to capitalize:

- the first letter of the word at the beginning of every sentence.
- proper names such as names of people, geographical names, company names, and names of organizations.
- days, months, and holidays.
- the word *I*.
- the first letter of a title such as the title of a movie or a book.
- the words in titles that have meaning (content words). Don't capitalize *a*, *an*, *the*, *and*, or prepositions such as *as* to, *for*, *of*, *from*, *at*, *in*, and *on*, unless they are the first word of a title (e.g., *The King and I*).

Punctuation

Keep the following rules in mind:

- Use a question mark (?) at the end of every question. Use a period (.) at the end of any sentence that is not a question.
- Exclamation marks (!), which indicate strong feelings such as surprise or joy, are generally not used in academic writing.
- Use commas (,) to separate a list of three or more things (*She speaks German, English, and Spanish*.).
- Use a comma after an introductory word or phrase. (*Although painful to humans, it is not deadly. / However, some species have fewer than 20 legs.*)
- Use a comma before a coordinating conjunction—*and*, *but*, *so*, *yet*, *or*, and *nor*—that joins two sentences (*Black widow bites are not usually deadly for adults, but they can be deadly for children*.).
- Use an apostrophe (') to show possession (*James's idea came from social networking sites*.).

- Use quotation marks (" ") to indicate the exact words used by someone else. (*In fact, Wesch says, "the Web is us."*)
- Use quotation marks to show when a word or phrase is being used in a special way, such as a definition. (*The name centipede means "100 legs."*)

Other Proofreading Tips:
- Print out your draft instead of reading it on your computer screen.
- Read your draft out loud. Use your finger or a pen to point to each word as you read it.
- Don't be afraid to mark up your draft. Use a colored pen to make corrections so you can see them easily when you write your next draft.
- Read your draft backwards—starting with the last word—to check your spelling. That way, you won't be distracted by the meaning.
- Have someone else read your draft and give you comments or ask you questions.
- Don't depend on a computer's spell-check. When the spell-check suggests a correction, make sure you agree with it before you accept the change.
- Remember to pay attention to the following items:
    - Short words such as *is*, *and*, *but*, *or*, *it*, *to*, *for*, *from*, and *so*.
    - Spelling of proper nouns.
    - Numbers and dates.
- Keep a list of spelling and grammar mistakes that you commonly make so that you can be aware of them as you edit your draft.

Watch out for frequently confused words:

- *there*, *their*, and *they're*
- *its* and *it's*
- *by*, *buy*, and *bye*
- *your* and *you're*
- *to*, *too*, and *two*
- *whose* and *who's*
- *where*, *wear*, *we're*, and *were*
- *then* and *than*
- *quit*, *quiet*, and *quite*
- *write* and *right*
- *affect* and *effect*
- *through*, *though*, and *thorough*
- *week* and *weak*
- *lose* and *loose*
- *accept* and *except*

Research and referencing

Using facts and quotes from journals and online sources will help to support your arguments in a written assignment. When you research information, you need to look for the most relevant and reliable sources. You will also need to provide appropriate citations for these sources; that is, you need to indicate that the words are not your own but rather come from someone else.

In academic writing, it is necessary for a writer to cite sources of all information that is not original. Using a source without citing it is known as **plagiarism**.

There are several ways to cite sources. Check with your teacher on the method or methods required at your institution.

Most institutions use the American Psychological Association (APA) or the Modern Language Association (MLA) format. Here are some examples of the APA format.

Book
Buettner, D. (2010). *Thrive: Finding happiness the blue zones way.* Washington, D.C.: National Geographic.

Blog Post
B C Howard. (2012, November 2). Are Facebook and Internet Addictions Affecting Our Minds? [Blog post]. Retrieved from http://newswatch.nationalgeographic.com/2012/11/02/are-facebook-and-internet-addictions-affecting-our-minds/

Magazine Article
White, M. (June 2011). Brimming Pools. *National Geographic*, 100-115.

Independent Student Handbook

Research Checklist

☐ Are my sources relevant to the assignment?

☐ Are my sources reliable? Think about the author and publisher. Ask yourself, "What is the author's point of view? Can I trust this information?"

☐ Have I noted all sources properly, including page numbers?

☐ When I am not citing a source directly, am I using my own words? In other words, am I using appropriate paraphrasing, which includes the use of synonyms, different word forms, and/or different grammatical structure?

☐ Are my sources up-to-date? Do they use the most recent data available? Having current sources is especially important for fields that change rapidly, such as technology and business.

☐ If I am using a direct quote, am I using the exact words that the person said or wrote?

☐ Am I using varied expressions for introducing citations, such as *According to X, As X says, X says / states / points out / explains . . .*?

Common signal phrases

Making an overview statement

It is generally agreed that . . .
It is clear (from the chart/table) that . . .
Generally, we can see that . . .

Giving supporting details and examples

One/An example (of this) is . . .
For example, . . . / For instance, . . .
Specifically, . . . / More specifically, . . .
From my experience, . . .

Giving reasons

This is due to . . .
This is because (of) . . .
One reason (for this) is . . .

Describing cause and effect

Consequently, . . . / Therefore, . . .
As a result, . . . /
As a consequence, . . .
This means that . . .
Because of this, . . .

Giving definitions

. . . which means . . .
In other words, . . .
That is . . .

Linking arguments and reasons

Furthermore, . . . / Moreover, . . .
In addition, . . . / Additionally, . . .
For one thing, . . . / For another example, . . .
Not only . . . but also . . .

Describing a process

First (of all), . . .
Then / Next / After that, . . .
As soon as . . . / When . . .
Finally, . . .

Outlining contrasting views

On the other hand, . . . / However, . . .
Although some people believe (that) . . ., it can also be argued that . . .
While it may be true that . . ., nevertheless, . . .
Despite this, . . . / Despite (the fact that) . . . Even though . . .

Softening a statement

It seems/appears that . . .
The evidence suggests/indicates that . . .

Giving a personal opinion

In my opinion, . . .
I (generally) agree that . . .
I think/feel that . . .
I believe (that) . . .

Restating/concluding

In conclusion, . . . / In summary, . . .
To conclude, . . . / To summarize, . . .

Independent Student Handbook

Reading and Writing Reference

Unit 3

Past Forms of Commonly Used Irregular Verbs

become—became	eat—ate	mean—meant
begin—began	feel—felt	meet—met
bend—bent	fight—fought	pay—paid
bet—bet	fall—fell	put—put
bite—bit	find—found	quit—quit
bleed—bled	fly—flew	read—read
blow—blew	forget—forgot	run—ran
build—built	get—got	say—said
break—broke	give—gave	see—saw
bring—brought	go—went	send—sent
burn—burned/burnt	grow—grew	sleep—slept
buy—bought	have—had	speak—spoke
catch—caught	hear—heard	spend—spent
choose—chose	hide—hid	stand—stood
come—came	hold—held	steal—stole
cost—cost	hurt—hurt	take—took
cut—cut	keep—kept	teach—taught
deal—dealt	know—knew	tell—told
dive—dove	lead—led	think—thought
do—did	leave—left	understand—understood
draw—drew	lie—lay	wear—wore
drink—drank	lose—lost	win—won
drive—drove	make—made	write—wrote

Vocabulary Index

Vocabulary Index

accommodate*	103
accumulate*	79
advocate*	96
alternative*	96
analysis*	26
approximate(ly)*	72
aspect*	50
attach*	26
authority*	11
collapse*	79
commission*	72
commit*	26
compact(ed)	79
comprise	33
concentration*	72
conduct*	33
conflict*	4
consequence(s)*	33
consistent	58
consumption*	58
convince(d)*	72
cooperate*	4
core*	96
crack	79
decade*	50
deduce*	26
demonstrate*	11
detective*	26
distinctive*	96
distribution*	4
dominate(d)*	103
dramatic(ally)*	103
dynamics*	4
emphatic*	72
enable*	50
enhance*	58
enormous*	96
eruption	79
establish*	11
examination	33
exceed*	50
expand*	96
explode	79
extract*	26
extraordinary	79
facilities	103
fee(s)*	103
focus*	50
function*	4
fundamental*	58
gender*	11
generate*	11
hierarchy*	4
identify*	26
identity	33
incentive*	103
income*	50
indicative*	72
inevitable*	50
infectious	33
infrastructure*	50
injure(d)*	72
institute*	50
intense*	11
interpret*	103
invest*	50
investigate*	26
justified*	58
majority	58
objective*	58
obtain*	33
partnership*	96
perception	4
period*	11
phenomenon*	58
pose*	103
predominant(ly)*	103
pressure	79
previous(ly)*	11
prime*	26
promote*	96
prone	72
psychologist*	11
range*	79
reliable	72
reluctant*	72
reveal*	4
rigid*	11
role*	4
sample	33
scholar	33
scope*	96
(self-)sufficient*	103
statistic(al)*	58
status*	4
suspect	26
sustain*	58
tend (to)	79
via*	96
vulnerable	33

*These words are on the Academic Word List (AWL). The AWL is a list of the 570 most frequent word families in academic texts. The list does not include words that are among the most frequent 2,000 words of English. For more information on the AWL, see http://www.victoria.ac.nz/lals/resources/academicwordlist/.

Academic Literacy Skills Index

Critical Thinking

Analyzing 19, 21, 31, 43, 45, 65, 67, 76, 86, 88, 100, 110

Applying information 9, 18, 31, 42, 56, 77, 101

Brainstorming 4, 17, 26, 32, 41, 50, 64, 72, 79, 87, 96, 103, 109

Discussing ideas 63, 108

Distinguishing fact from speculation 30, 40

Evaluating 8, 16, 55, 63, 76

Inference 40, 108

Making connections/comparisons 2, 24, 48, 70

Peer Evaluation 68, 91, 113

Personalizing/Reflecting 1, 8, 23, 47, 55, 69, 93, 94, 100

Predicting content 4, 11, 26, 32, 50, 58, 72, 79, 96, 103

Synthesizing 10, 16, 32, 40, 57, 63, 78, 86, 102, 108

Thinking ahead 10, 32, 57, 78, 102

Reading Skills/Strategies

Identifying key details 8, 30, 54, 76, 85

Identifying supporting ideas/details 8, 16, 39, 63, 100, 108

Identifying the main idea 8, 9, 15, 30, 39, 54, 62, 76, 85, 100, 107

Identifying:

- cause and effect 101, 108
- sequence 40
- parts of an opinion paragraph 42
- reasons 63, 76

Inferring meaning from context 15, 39, 62, 85, 107

Organizing your notes 77

Understanding reasons 56, 77

Vocabulary Skills

Building vocabulary 4, 11, 26, 32, 50, 58, 72, 79, 96, 103

Using a dictionary 10, 32, 57, 78, 102

Using vocabulary 4, 11, 26, 32, 50, 58, 72, 79, 96, 103

Writing Skills

Editing for language mistakes 22, 46, 68, 92, 114

Free writing 17, 41, 64, 87, 109

Planning and creating an outline 44, 66, 89, 111

Revising a draft 20, 22, 44, 46, 67, 68, 90, 112

Reviewing paragraph writing 19

Taking notes 77

Writing a draft 44, 66, 89, 111

Writing a topic sentence 66

Writing a well-developed paragraph 110

Writing an introductory paragraph 87

Writing a paragraph with main and supporting ideas 43, 66

Visual Literacy

Interpreting graphic information:

- graphs and charts 94
- infographics 52, 81, 84, 86

Academic Literacy Skills Index

- maps 49, 70, 84, 95

Using graphic organizers:

- concept maps 44, 45, 77
- process diagram 86
- T-charts 76, 87, 101, 108
- Venn diagrams 20, 21
- timeline 77

Test-Taking Skills

Categorizing and classifying 40, 76, 100, 108

Chart and diagram completion 8, 20, 30, 76

Choosing correct options 54, 62, 72

Filling in missing details 4, 15, 16, 26, 33, 42, 58, 85, 96, 103

Matching questions 11, 50, 76, 79, 107

Notes and summary completion 8, 30, 76

Sequencing 31, 40, 86

Short answer questions 4, 8, 11, 16, 26, 33, 39, 50, 54, 56, 58, 63, 72, 79, 85, 86, 96, 103, 108

yes/no/not given questions 21, 45

Language for Writing

Making Comparisons 17

Parallelism 87

Review of modals of obligation and possibility 41

Using *If . . ., (then) . . .* 109

Using the simple past and *used to* 64

Acknowledgments

The authors and publisher would like to thank the following reviewers for their help during the development of this series:

UNITED STATES AND CANADA

Gokhan Alkanat, Auburn University at Montgomery, AL; Nikki Ashcraft, Shenandoah University, VA; Karin Avila-John, University of Dayton, OH; John Baker, Oakland Community College, MI; Shirley Baker, Alliant International University, CA; Michelle Bell, University of South Florida, FL; Nancy Boyer, Golden West College, CA; Kathy Brenner, BU/CELOP, Mattapan, MA; Janna Brink, Mt. San Antonio College, Chino Hills, CA; Carol Brutza, Gateway Community College, CT; Sarah Camp, University of Kentucky, Center for ESL, KY; Maria Caratini, Eastfield College, TX; Ana Maria Cepero, Miami Dade College, Miami, FL; Daniel Chaboya, Tulsa Community College, OK; Patricia Chukwueke, English Language Institute – UCSD Extension, CA; Julia A. Correia, Henderson State University, CT; Suzanne Crisci, Bunker Hill Community College, MA; Lina Crocker, University of Kentucky, Lexington, KY; Katie Crowder, University of North Texas, TX; Joe Cunningham, Park University, Kansas City, MO; Lynda Dalgish, Concordia College, NY; Jeffrey Diluglio, Center for English Language and Orientation Programs: Boston University, MA; Scott Dirks, Kaplan International Center at Harvard Square, MA; Kathleen Dixon, SUNY Stony Brook - Intensive English Center, Stony Brook, NY; Margo Downey, Boston University, Boston, MA; John Drezek, Richland College, TX; Qian Du, Ohio State University, Columbus, OH; Leslie Kosel Eckstein, Hillsborough Community College, FL; Anwar El-Issa, Antelope Valley College, CA; Beth Kozbial Ernst, University of Wisconsin-Eau Claire, WI; Anrisa Fannin, The International Education Center at Diablo Valley College, CA; Jennie Farnell, Greenwich Japanese School, Greenwich, CT; Rosa Vasquez Fernandez, John F. Kennedy, Institute Of Languages, Inc., Boston, MA; Mark Fisher, Lone Star College, TX; Celeste Flowers, University of Central Arkansas, AR; John Fox, English Language Institute, GA; Pradel R. Frank, Miami Dade College, FL; Sherri Fujita, Hawaii Community College, Hilo, HI; Sally Gearheart, Santa Rosa Jr. College, CA; Elizabeth Gillstrom, The University of Pennsylvania, Philadelphia, PA; Sheila Goldstein, Rockland Community College, Brentwood, NY; Karen Grubbs, ELS Language Centers, FL; Sudeepa Gulati, long beach city college, Torrance, CA; Joni Hagigeorges, Salem State University, MA; Marcia Peoples Halio, English Language Institute, University of Delaware, DE; Kara Hanson, Oregon State University, Corvallis, OR; Suha Hattab, Triton College, Chicago, IL; Marla Heath, Sacred Heart Univiversity and Norwalk Community College, Stamford, CT; Valerie Heming, University of Central Missouri, MO; Mary Hill, North Shore Community College, MA; Harry Holden, North Lake College, Dallas, TX; Ingrid Holm, University of Massachusetts Amherst, MA; Katie Hurter, Lone Star College – North Harris, TX; Barbara Inerfeld, Program in American Language Studies (PALS) Rutgers University/New Brunswick, Piscataway, NJ; Justin Jernigan, Georgia Gwinnett College, GA; Barbara Jonckheere, ALI/CSULB, Long Beach, CA; Susan Jordan, Fisher College, MA; Maria Kasparova, Bergen Community College, NJ; Maureen Kelbert, Vancouver Community College, Surrey, BC, Canada; Gail Kellersberger, University of Houston-Downtown, TX; David Kent, Troy University, Goshen, AL; Daryl Kinney, Los Angeles City College, CA; Jennifer Lacroix, Center for English Language and Orientation Programs: Boston University, MA; Stuart Landers, Misouri State University, Springfield, MO; Mary Jo Fletcher LaRocco, Ph.D., Salve Regina University, Newport, RI; Bea Lawn, Gavilan College, Gilroy, CA; Margaret V. Layton, University of Nevada, Reno Intensive English Language Center, NV; Alice Lee, Richland College, Mesquite, TX; Heidi Lieb, Bergen Community College, NJ; Kerry Linder, Language Studies International New York, NY; Jenifer Lucas-Uygun, Passaic County Community College, Paterson, NJ; Alison MacAdams, Approach International Student Center, MA; Julia MacDonald, Brock University, Saint Catharines, ON, Canada; Craig Machado, Norwalk Community College, CT; Andrew J. MacNeill, Southwestern College, CA; Melanie A. Majeski, Naugatuck Valley Community College, CT; Wendy Maloney, College of DuPage, Aurora, IL; Chris Mares, University of Maine – Intensive English Institute, Maine; Josefina Mark, Union County College, NJ; Connie Mathews, Nashville State Community College, TN; Bette Matthews, Mid-Pacific Institute, HI; Richard McDorman, inlingua Language Centers (Miami, FL) and Pennsylvania State University, Pompano Beach, FL; Sara McKinnon, College of Marin, CA; Christine Mekkaoui, Pittsburg State University, KS; Holly A. Milkowart, Johnson County Community College, KS; Donna Moore, Hawaii Community College, Hilo, HI; Ruth W. Moore, International English Center, University of Colorado at Boulder, CO; Kimberly McGrath Moreira, University of Miami, FL; Warren Mosher, University of Miami, FL; Sarah Moyer, California State University Long Beach, CA; Lukas Murphy, Westchester Community College, NY; Elena Nehrebecki, Hudson Community College, NJ; Bjarne Nielsen, Central Piedmont Community College, North Carolina; David Nippoldt, Reedley College, CA; Nancy Nystrom, University Of Texas At San Antonio, Austin, TX; Jane O'Connor, Emory College, Atlanta, GA; Daniel E. Opacki, SIT Graduate Institute, Brattleboro, VT; Lucia Parsley, Virginia Commonwealth University, VA; Wendy Patriquin, Parkland College, IL; Nancy Pendleton, Cape Cod Community College, Attleboro, MA; Marion Piccolomini, Communicate With Ease, LTD, PA, Barbara Pijan, Portland State University, Portland, OR, Marjorie Pitts, Ohio Northern University, Ada, OH; Carolyn Prager, Spanish-American Institute, NY; Eileen Prince, Prince Language Associates Incorporated, MA; Sema Pulak, Texas A & M University, TX; Mary Kay Purcell, University of Evansville, Evansville, IN; Christina Quartararo, St. John's University, Jamaica, NY; James T. Raby, Clark University, MA; Anouchka Rachelson, Miami-Dade College, FL; Sherry Rasmussen, DePaul University, IL; Amy Renehan, University of Washington, WA; Daniel Rivas, Irvine Valley College, Irvine, CA; Esther Robbins, Prince George's Community College, PA; Bruce Rogers, Spring International Language Center at Arapahoe College, Littleton, CO; Helen Roland, Miami Dade College, FL; Linda Roth, Vanderbilt University English Language Center, TN; Janine Rudnick, El Paso Community College, TX; Paula Sanchez, Miami Dade College – Kendall Campus, FL; Deborah Sandstrom, Tutorium in Intensive English at University of Illinois at Chicago, Elmhurst, IL; Marianne Hsu Santelli, Middlesex County College, NJ; Elena Sapp, INTO Oregon State University, Corvallis, OR; Alice Savage, Lone Star College System: North Harris, TX; Jitana Schaefer, Pensacola State College, Pensacola, FL; Lynn Ramage Schaefer, University of Central Arkansas, AR; Ann Schroth, Johnson & Wales University, Dayville, CT;

Acknowledgments

Margaret Shippey, Miami Dade College, FL; Lisa Sieg, Murray State University, KY; Samanthia Slaight, North Lake College, Richardson, TX; Ann Snider, UNK University of NE Kearney, Kearney, NE; Alison Stamps, ESL Center at Mississippi State University, Mississippi; Peggy Street, ELS Language Centers, Miami, FL; Lydia Streiter, York College Adult Learning Center, NY; Steve Strizver, Miami Beach, FL; Nicholas Taggart, Arkansas State University, AR; Marcia Takacs, Coastline Community College, CA; Tamara Teffeteller, University of California Los Angeles, American Language Center, CA; Adrianne Aiko Thompson, Miami Dade College, Miami, FL; Rebecca Toner, English Language Programs, University of Pennsylvania, PA; Evina Baquiran Torres, Zoni Language Centers, NY; William G. Trudeau, Missouri Southern State University, MO; Troy Tucker, Edison State College, FL; Maria Vargas-O'Neel, Miami Dade College, FL; Amerca Vazquez, Miami Dade College, FL; Alison Vinande, Modesto Junior College, CA; Christie Ward, IELP, Central CT State University, Hartford, CT; Colin Ward, Lone Star College - North Harris, Houston, TX; Denise Warner, Lansing Community College, Lansing, MI; Rita Rutkowski Weber, University of Wisconsin – Milwaukee, WI; James Wilson, Cosumnes River College, Sacramento, CA; Dolores "Lorrie" Winter, California State University Fullerton, Buena Park, CA; Wendy Wish-Bogue, Valencia Community College, FL; Cissy Wong, Sacramento City College, CA; Sarah Worthington, Tucson, Arizona; Kimberly Yoder, Kent State University, ESL Center, OH.

ASIA

Nor Azni Abdullah, Universiti Teknologi Mara; Morgan Bapst, Seoul National University of Science and Technology; Herman Bartelen, Kanda Institute of Foreign Languages, Sano; Maiko Berger, Ritsumeikan Asia Pacific University; Thomas E. Bieri, Nagoya College; Paul Bournhonesque, Seoul National University of Technology; Joyce Cheah Kim Sim, Taylor's University, Selangor Darul Ehsan; Michael C. Cheng, National Chengchi University; Fu-Dong Chiou, National Taiwan University; Derek Currie, Korea University, Sejong Institute of Foreign Language Studies; Wendy Gough, St. Mary College/Nunoike Gaigo Senmon Gakko, Ichinomiya; Christoph A. Hafner, City University of Hong Kong; Monica Hamciuc, Ritsumeikan Asia-Pacific University, Kagoshima; Rob Higgens, Ritsumeikan University; Wenhua Hsu, I-Shou University; Lawrie Hunter, Kochi University of Technology; Helen Huntley, Hanoi University; Debra Jones, Tokyo Woman's Christian University, Tokyo; Shih Fan Kao, JinWen University of Science and Technology; Ikuko Kashiwabara, Osaka Electro-Communication University; Alyssa Kim, Hankuk University of Foreign Studies; Richard S. Lavin, Prefecturla University of Kumamoto; Mike Lay, American Institute Cambodia; Byoung-Kyo Lee, Yonsei University; Lin Li, Capital Normal University, Beijing; Bien Thi Thanh Mai, The International University – Vietnam National University, Ho Chi Minh City; Hudson Murrell, Baiko Gakuin University; Keiichi Narita, Niigata University; Orapin Nasawang, Udon Thani Rajabhat University; Huynh Thi Ai Nguyen, Vietnam USA Society; James Pham, IDP Phnom Penh; John Racine, Dokkyo University; Duncan Rose, British Council Singapore; Greg Rouault, Konan University, Hirao School of Management, Osaka; Simone Samuels, The Indonesia Australia Language Foundation, Jakarta; Yuko Shimizu, Ritsumeikan University; Wang Songmei, Beijing Institute of Education Faculty; Richmond Stroupe, Soka University; Peechaya Suriyawong, Udon Thani Rajabhat University; Teoh Swee Ai, Universiti Teknologi Mara; Chien-Wen Jenny Tseng, National Sun Yat-Sen University; Hajime Uematsu, Hirosaki University; Sy Vanna, Newton Thilay School, Phnom Penh; Matthew Watterson, Hongik University; Anthony Zak, English Language Center, Shantou University.

LATIN AMERICA AND THE CARIBBEAN

Ramon Aguilar, Universidad Tecnológica de Hermosillo, México; Lívia de Araújo Donnini Rodrigues, University of São Paulo, Brazil; Cecilia Avila, Universidad de Xapala, México; Beth Bartlett, Centro Cultural Colombo Americano, Cali, Colombia; Raúl Billini, Colegio Loyola, Dominican Republic; Nohora Edith Bryan, Universidad de La Sabana, Colombia; Raquel Hernández Cantú, Instituto Tecnológico de Monterrey, Mexico; Millie Commander, Inter American University of Puerto Rico, Puerto Rico; José Alonso Gaxiola Soto, CEI Universidad Autonoma de Sinaloa, Mazatlán, Mexico; Raquel Hernandez, Tecnologico de Monterrey, Mexico; Edwin Marín-Arroyo, Instituto Tecnológico de Costa Rica; Rosario Mena, Instituto Cultural Dominico-Americano, Dominican Republic; Elizabeth Ortiz Lozada, COPEI-COPOL English Institute, Ecuador; Gilberto Rios Zamora, Sinaloa State Language Center, Mexico; Patricia Veciños, El Instituto Cultural Argentino Norteamericano, Argentina; Isabela Villas Boas, Casa Thomas Jefferson, Brasília, Brazil; Roxana Viñes, Language Two School of English, Argentina.

EUROPE, MIDDLE EAST, AND NORTH AFRICA

Tom Farkas, American University of Cairo, Egypt; Ghada Hozayen, Arab Academy for Science, Technology and Maritime Transport, Egypt; Tamara Jones, ESL Instructor, SHAPE Language Center, Belgium; Jodi Lefort, Sultan Qaboos University, Muscat, Oman; Neil McBeath, Sultan Qaboos University, Oman; Barbara R. Reimer, CERTESL, UAE University, UAE; Nashwa Nashaat Sobhy, The American University in Cairo, Egypt; Virginia Van Hest-Bastaki, Kuwait University, Kuwait.

AUSTRALIA

Susan Austin, University of South Australia, Joanne Cummins, Swinburne College; Pamela Humphreys, Griffith University.

Special thanks to Diego Asencio, Lucky Chhetri, Susan Hough, Caitlin O'Connell Rodwell, Aydogan Ozcan, Alison Wright, and Richard Wurman for their kind assistance during this book's development.

This series is dedicated to Kristin L. Johannsen, whose love for the world's cultures and concern for the world's environment were an inspiration to family, friends, students, and colleagues.